SELECTING THE
CHURCH
COMPUTER

SELECTING THE
CHURCH
COMPUTER

WILLIAM R. JOHNSON

Abingdon Press
Nashville

SELECTING THE CHURCH COMPUTER

Copyright © 1984 by Abingdon Press

Scripture quotations are from the Revised Standard Version of the
Bible, copyrighted 1946, 1952, © 1971, 1973 by the Division of Christian
Education of the National Council of Churches of Christ in the U.S.A.,
and are used by permission. The Extended Binary Coded Decimal
Interchange Code (EBCDIC) is reprinted on pages 133-36 with permis-
sion of the International Business Machines Corporation. The American
Standard Code for Information Interchange (ASCII) is reprinted on
pages 131-33 with permission from American National Standard X3.4-
1977, copyright 1977 by the American National Standards Institute.
Copies of this standard may be purchased from the American National
Standards Institute at 1430 Broadway, New York, N.Y. 10018.

Library of Congress Cataloging in Publication Data

JOHNSON, WILLIAM R. (William Raymond), 1951-
  Selecting the church computer.
  Includes index.
  1. Church work—Data processing. 2. Electronic
  digital computers. I. Title.
  BV625.77.J64   1984   254'.0028'54   84-9356

ISBN 0-687-37135-X

MANUFACTURED BY THE PARTHENON PRESS AT
NASHVILLE, TENNESSEE, UNITED STATES OF AMERICA

To . . .

Ann, without whose love and encouragement this book would not have been written

Sarah and Seth, in whose lifetimes computerized Christendom will become a reality

Acknowledgments

I wish to acknowledge my indebtedness and thanksgiving to the following individuals and groups that, through their collective resources, helped make this book possible:

Ann Johnson, wife and confidante, who laughs when I laugh, cries when I cry, and who knows when to listen with divine patience.

Kayo Suzukida, secretary and friend, whose mastery of the English language assisted me to write with greater relevancy for computer laypersons.

The Reverend Albert E. Fifhause, associate and friend, who offered much needed constructive criticism of my writing through his unique combination of technical background and theological training.

L. Ted Stephan of MAI/Basic Four Information Systems, who arranged for me to use a Basic Four S/10 micro-computer word processing system in my home during the final phases of the book's development.

The congregations of Greeley United Methodist Church of Greeley, Iowa; St. Paul's United Methodist Church of Waukon, Iowa; and St. John's United Methodist Church of Dorchester, Iowa; whose members ministered to me, nurtured me, loved me, and allowed me the privilege of learning the meaning of the word *pastor*.

To these and countless others, I am humbly grateful.

Bill (William R. Johnson)

Contents

SELECTING THE
CHURCH COMPUTER

Chapter 1

IN THE BEGINNING

The beautiful account of creation found in the first chapter of Genesis teaches humankind of its stewardship responsibilities to the "heaven and earth." God created it and pronounced it good. He gave humankind the power to think. He taught humanity to probe the heavens and earth and gave the gift of learning and knowledge that he expects to be used wisely. However, when God created the place human beings call home, did he know what the gift of increasing knowledge would bring in the twentieth century? Did he have any inkling that with the passing of time his children would be using a creation of humankind's knowledge called the computer to complete his work?

It is, of course, possible to speculate upon what God knew or foresaw about technology when he created humanity. Whether God knew about computers in the twentieth century or not is an academic question, best left to seminary students and theologians for debate. Computers are here, and they are here to stay.

Computers are changing society in ways never imagined by science fiction writers of only fifty years ago. A cybernetic revolution is occurring throughout the world that rivals the industrial revolution of the 1800s. The church of Jesus Christ, as part of society, cannot escape and is challenged by the technological metamorphosis occurring today. The transformation being experienced by the church now and in the future may become one of the most significant events since the

Reformation. The impact of computers in the church is giving birth to computerized Christendom.

The computer world can be a baffling, frustrating, confusing place. It uses a foreign language often called "computerese." This can confound even the most brilliantly trained theologian to the everyday parish pastor or full-time church worker. When facing the dilemma of learning a wholly new and different language to communicate in a strange, new world, full-time church workers frequently wonder if it's worth the effort. "Why can't we go on like we used to," is the often heard cry.

Is it really necessary for full-time lay and clergy workers in the church to receive a baptism into the technological maze of computers? It would seem that the answer is yes. Whether the church wants to or not, it must minister to a technologically dependent, computer-oriented society. If Christians do not learn about computer technologies, the twenty-first century church will lose its ministering ability in a cybernetic society. In addition, the benefits of automated information control can improve the work of Christ's church through better steward-ship of its human resources. By utilizing those amazing devices called computers, the church can discover new methods of ministering to a cybernetic society while increasing the effective utilization of its information at the same time.

The purpose of this book is to equip the church with the knowledge of planning for and using computers in its ministry. An attempt is made in the following pages to:
1. Discuss some of the fundamental issues surrounding church computers.
2. Provide a brief introduction to computerese.
3. Illustrate some of the many practical church computer applications.
4. Suggest a generalized plan for selecting and installing a church computer.
5. Introduce how computers may be used in the church school.
6. Reflect upon the linkage between technology and theology.

A Brief History of Computers

Today it is no secret that computers and their related technologies are infiltrating every aspect of our lives. Society has been permeated by these fascinating devices. They are rapidly entering every field of endeavor and filling our minds with new ideas. The computer revolution is producing an explosion of knowledge never before experienced in the history of humankind. However, all revolutions had beginnings, and computers found their humble start in England.

In 1833, a Cambridge University mathematician named Charles Babbage proposed a computing device called the "analytical engine." As with so many great inventors in history, he was ridiculed for even suggesting a machine that could compute when people could do it just as easily with paper and pencil. In many ways, he can be considered the historical parent of modern day computers even though "Babbage's folly" was never actually built.

Following Babbage over one hundred years later was Harvard Professor Howard Aiken, who constructed the world's first digital computer. A digital computer is essentially a machine that counts very rapidly. This device was called the Mark I. In 1937, Aiken started to build the machine and completed it in 1944. The Mark I was a marvel for its day, being controlled automatically with electromagnetic relays. However, this computer was essentially a mechanical device.

The first *electronic* digital computer was built between 1939 and 1946 at the University of Pennsylvania as a secret wartime machine to perform the complex calculations of artillery trajectories. This machine was called the Electronic Numerical Integrator and Calculator, or ENIAC. The ENIAC had between 19,000 and 20,000 vacuum tubes and did not have relays as the Mark I had. It weighed over thirty tons and used about 1,500 square feet of floor space. ENIAC could reduce the time required for the trajectory calculations from three hundred days by hand to slightly less than one day. The designers of this first electronic computer were J. Presper Eckert, Jr. and John W. Mauchly.

Before completing the ENIAC in 1952, Eckert and Mauchly conceived the idea for a second major electronic computer named EDVAC, or Electronic Discrete Variable Automatic Computer. However, the two inventors delayed EDVAC's development to begin history's first computer company, Universal Automatic Computer, popularly known as UNIVAC. Because of this delay, the EDSAC (Electronic Discrete Stored Automatic Computer) was completed in 1949 at Cambridge University and became the second electronic computer in history. The EDSAC holds the honor of being the first computer capable of actually storing information in an electronic memory.

Although the EDSAC was completed before the EDVAC, EDVAC's design became the forerunner of the UNIVAC-1 computer. The UNIVAC-1 was finished in 1951, sold to the United States government, and made operational in the Bureau of the Census. The first business computer was another UNIVAC-1 purchased by General Electric in Louisville, Kentucky, and installed in 1954.

After this early period, several other computer companies were formed including International Business Machines, now famous as IBM. These enterprises manufactured the world's "first generation" computers and sold them to large businesses. From that point, the computer industry exploded into a multibillion dollar business that has spawned the newest generation of inexpensive small microcomputers on the market today.

In the last fifteen years these amazing technological marvels have appeared in grocery stores, hospitals, schools as early as kindergarten and first grade, and even in gas stations. In the future, you will be able to drive a car into a service station, insert a specially coded magnetic card with a personalized secret number, pump gasoline into the car, and the cost will be charged automatically against your bank account. All this will occur through computers. No human interaction will be required, and no actual cash will be exchanged.

Computers in the Present Day Church

With computers finding their way into such everyday occurrences as pumping gas, it is inevitable that they should appear in the sacred halls of Christendom. Most mainline Christian denominations use computers in a variety of ways. Judicatory bodies through local churches have purchased or leased every conceivable size of computer. For example, in the United Methodist Church, sixty-six annual conferences use computers in some way, shape, or form. (An annual conference is a judicatory body consisting of between 150 and 1,500 local churches.) Among the United Methodist general agencies, there are more than fifteen computer installations from small microcomputers to large mainframe computers. Accurate statistics for computer infiltration in local churches are not yet available; however, most large denominations report significant interest.

The existing church computers in denominational offices are used for a variety of applications. A few of these are:

1. Mailing lists and directories with label generation.
2. Media resource center control including bookings, catalog generation, inventory, indexing, and book-keeping.
3. Camp information control including registration and bookkeeping.
4. Meeting registration for medium and large judicatory gatherings.
5. Statistical and demographic information plus statistical analysis.
6. Pastor profile information used to assist in the placement of ordained clergy in churches.

7. Fiscal accounting including general ledger, remittances, disbursements, insurance billings, pensions, budgeting, payroll, automatic check writing, church loan control, investment control, auditing, and capital fund drive control.
8. Credit union functions.
9. Church foundation functions including financial investment controls, donor lists, and property inventory.
10. Talent bank information for better utilization of human resources.
11. Word processing including personalized mass mailings, camera-ready copy of judicatory reports for publication, and general document production.

As you can see from the abbreviated list above, the church of Jesus Christ at national and regional levels has been heavily penetrated by these new tools. The computer is rapidly becoming the chief tool of information control in many denominations.

Several years ago, the question about computers in the local church revolved around the probability and possibility of getting one. The question today is not "if," but "when" a computer will be obtained in a local church. The computer/cybernetic/information age has dawned upon Christendom and exists whether Christians want it or not.

As the church begins to use new technologies, the point to remember is that any computer is simply a *tool*. It is not the panacea that will save the church from all its ills. It is not the second coming of Jesus Christ as some church computer experts seem to believe. It is not an idol to be worshiped. It is just a tool. When appropriately used, it is a tool that can significantly enhance the church's ministry on a practical, human level.

Chapter 2

DEMYTHOLOGIZING THE COMPUTER

Even if you have not previously been exposed to computers, societal notions and comments may have subconsciously shaped your views about them. Some of these preconceived notions are probably true and some, more than likely, are false. Regardless of your position in the church, the opinions you express about computers will have some impact upon the effective foundation of using a computer to improve your church's ministry. Thus, it may help you if I demythologize the computer before discussing its practical applications in the church.

There are four technological myths that could prevent your church from using a computer:

1. **Computers are difficult to use.**
   - Computers are NOT difficult to use. From the operator's point of view, most of today's computers are easy to use and guide the user through the necessary steps to process and extract needed information.
   - Modern computers, especially microcomputers, are considered *user friendly*. A user friendly computer always asks the user what he or she wants to do next. An operator simply follows the "prompts" or questions, and responds to them appropriately. The computer will tell you if your response doesn't make sense or if it needs more information. Ideally, a user friendly computer will never leave you without a choice or option. In case a problem occurs, a user friendly

computer generally provides a way for you to get back to the very beginning of the task. In addition, a user friendly machine usually has a "help" function, whereby the operator can type a "?" or the word "HELP," and the computer will assist with a possible answer to the question.

2. **You have to be a genius to use it.**

   • A person doesn't have to be a mathematical genius or an electronic wizard to USE a computer. Computers today are designed to function with kindergarten and first grade children of average intelligence at the keyboard. Some aspects of computers do require a rudimentary knowledge of math, algebra, and a computer language, but to use a computer in your church work, mathematical expertise is not a prerequisite. Simply being able to respond intelligently to questions and prompts is what a person needs, not the knowledge of a genius.

3. **It's the computer's fault.**

   • When an error or mistake occurs, very seldom is it the computer's fault. There is a saying in the computer world designated by *GIGO* that has its origins in the very early days of computers. GIGO is an acronym for "garbage in/garbage out." When anyone puts garbage into a computer, it returns garbage as output. Why? Because computers are extremely reliable and DO EXACTLY WHAT THEY ARE TOLD TO DO.

   • When you have had a problem with an insurance bill or bank statement, how often have you been apologetically told by the firm's representative, "It's the computer's fault"? It is a human tendency not to admit mistakes and blame someone else for our errors. What better scapegoat is there than an impersonal machine that can't defend itself?

   • When something does malfunction in a computer, 99 percent of the time it is due to human error. It is fallible

DEMYTHOLOGIZING THE COMPUTER

human beings who program computers or enter the data that make the mistakes. Everyday persons with families, mortgages, and two cars in the garage operate the computers on which humankind is so dependent and make the errors that cause the problems for so many other everyday folks. When discussing computers, remember that it is very seldom the computer's fault because it does exactly what it has been programmed to do.

4. **Computers are "smart."**
   - Computers are *not* smart. In fact, they are quite dumb. It is important to remember that when you work with a computer, you are really working with a machine. A machine that is literally stupid, obeying only the user's commands, not accomplishing anything unless it is told to do something by a person.
   - The machines and computers created in Hollywood movie studios to "take over the world" are several years down the technological path. You will be hearing more about these artificially intelligent or heuristic computers in the late 1980s and 1990s. This kind of computer will have the ability to think or learn from its mistakes. Such computers do exist today, but only in the laboratory and experimental phase. About 1990, these computers will appear regularly in the market place with a quite substantial cost. Eventually, however, a computer with artificial intelligence will be affordable and practical for a church or home.
   - Any present day computer, however, is a marvelous, stupendous, fantastic, and *very dumb* number and word cruncher. A dumb tool, the computer produces desired information in specified forms when it is needed.

If you have *cyberphobia*, i.e., fear of computers, just reading this chapter will not remove your fears. Even if you aren't afraid of computers, but don't agree with what has been said about computer myths, these words will not cause you to believe computers are just simply tools. The only way to alleviate your discomfort is to actually use a computer. Find out what the machine will *and* won't do by using one in a relaxed environment.

It would be better to avoid experimenting with a computer in your local computer store. This is because the sales representative will lead you through preprogrammed demonstrations that really don't allow customers to relieve their tensions about the machines. It's very difficult to really understand computers when a well-meaning sales person keeps extolling the virtues of the particular machine you are using.

The place to try a computer is at your local library or school. Many public libraries are installing small computers for their patrons to learn about and use. Most high schools, junior highs, and even some elementary schools have computers that can be used after school and on weekends. You could use the school computers to learn about this new tool's usefulness for you and the church. Another possibility would be to take an evening continuing education course introducing computers and their potential. Any of these opportunities would provide practical experience using a computer and hopefully reduce any emotional discomfort or tension you may feel about the machines.

It is generally true that you can't hurt the computer. Experimentation with responses to questions and prompts will provide you with a much better understanding of the computer's limitations and potential. In the rare instance that something you try does cause a problem, there are always professionals to assist you. Computers are very difficult to break, even if you set out to do so.

In essence, technological demythologizing is knowing that you don't need to be fearful of experimenting with a computer. It means discovering the confidence to see how a computer responds and what it can do for you and your church.

Chapter 3

CHURCH MANAGEMENT INFORMATION: THE TOOL OF THE TRADE

The church of Jesus Christ is his body present in the world for his work. The work of Christ has not been and will never be an easy task. Those who believe that God's mission is confined to the walls of church buildings frequently believe that God's work occurs only in those buildings. In other words, there are those who presume the Body of Christ can only be found in church buildings. Such mistaken belief results from many factors—the most important of which may be the lack of proper information required for the Lord's work.

Adequate management, administration, and organization of the church's mission require clear, precise, and concise information. If the church has more accurate information about the needs, dreams, talents, and lives of the people it serves, its ministry will be more effective. In other words, for church workers to become more capable disciples and better stewards of the church's resources, an increasing level of ministry management information is required.

Management Information Systems in the Church

The concept of good administrative church data is essentially an application of an automation technique called *management information systems* (MIS). MIS is a notion revolving around computers that developed in the late 1960s and early 1970s. A management information system uses external and internal organizational information to generate more effective and efficient management (administration) of the organization. If the purpose of MIS is achieved, then the work of the organization is improved and benefits those affected by the work of the organization.

As you might surmise, the major tool of MIS is the computer. MIS is not limited to computers and could involve other technologies such as copy machines, video tape recorders, telephone systems, microfiche equipment, and other modern technological advancements. However, MIS does tend to utilize the computer as its main tool, placing all fundamental and often crucial information control in one or more computing devices.

MIS in the church means that a process is followed whereby available information is used to increase the effectiveness of our ministry. If MIS is used properly, ministry enhancement occurs not only in our own communities, but also throughout the world. Thus, if your church installs a computer, it will be used to create better stewardship of your church's information—a Management Information System.

MIS is essentially a combination of data processing and word processing functions, both of which may occur with a computer's assistance. To assist you further in grasping MIS, the following paragraphs define *data* and *word processing*.

Data Processing

Data processing (DP) in a pure sense is a function that every person engages in at every moment of each day. Data processing is an act of receiving information, manipulating it in various ways, and reporting that information in comprehendible terms.

Quite frequently today, data processing is associated *only* with computers. However, it should not be confined to them. Any common everyday occurrence that requires information to make a decision or achieve an end result can be considered data processing. For example, if you balance your checkbook through a manual system, you are engaged in data processing. DP is used whenever you follow a recipe using instructions passed down from your grandparents to produce the final, delicious result. DP is also used when you build a coffee table in a basement woodworking shop by following blueprint plans.

Electronic data processing (EDP) uses an electronic device to assist with the storage and manipulation of the information into a useable form. The electronic device could be a computer or a calculator, but EDP generally *does* refer to using a computer. An example of EDP in a church would be entering pledge information about church members into the computer and then using the machine to provide year-to-date data about how well the members are doing with their contributions.

Word Processing

Word processing (WP) is the manipulation of characters, words, phrases, paragraphs, and pages of text so that letters, reports, and other printed documents may be produced in an easy and efficient manner. Word processing generally refers to using a computer for document production; however, word processing can also use a standard typewriter as a tool.

An example of word processing in a local church would be a personalized letter from the pastor concerning the yearly financial appeal. This letter would be designed for all church members, and its contents might be exactly the same for everyone. However, the pastor has the desire to personalize it. If the church secretary types this letter and the church has five hundred families, the secretary would have to "keyboard" five hundred letters and envelopes to achieve personalization.

Through the computer, the name, address, and salutation can be easily inserted at the beginning of each letter. In addition, the computer can place the family's or person's name within the body of the letter as desired. For example, if the pastor is good friends with a certain family or person in the

25

congregation, the computer can print "Dear Dave and Mary" in the salutation. On the other hand, if the pastor is not familiar with a particular family, the computer can print "Dear Mr. and Mrs. Robinson."

Using the power of computer word processing in the above example means the secretary types the letter ONLY ONCE! The computer does the rest. In churches where the pastor is also the secretary, enormous amounts of time can be saved in such instances. Obviously, this creates more time for the pastor to analyze the church's information and respond more rapidly to human needs.

DP and WP as Part of MIS

The concepts of data and word processing described above are shared in the MIS concept. Diagram 3-1 gives a simple visual illustration of MIS.

Diagram 3-1

MANAGEMENT INFORMATION SYSTEMS

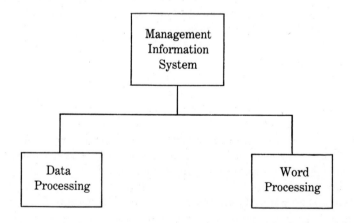

In conclusion, a management information system in a local church can:

1. Make the congregation more aware of real ministry needs.
2. Provide additional time for the real work of the church—by enabling church folks to react more quickly to human need and suffering.
3. Create a more effective mission in the church.
4. Produce efficient stewardship of all church resources, human and monetary.

A key to better ministry in future decades is the development and implementation of church management information systems. This is the tool of the trade, and the tool of the tool is the computer.

Chapter 4

A FOREIGN LANGUAGE CALLED "COMPUTERESE"

Communicating in computerized Christendom or, for that matter, in an automated society can be a major problem for the uninitiated. Those who do not have the knowledge of computer terms and dialects often find themselves left out of conversations, which leaves an empty, frustrating feeling. Computer neophytes feel left out and abandoned as if the world is passing them by with an agenda of which they have no part. This is primarily because the general language of the computer world is a baffling array of strange sounding terms and phrases that frequently seem to be straight from a science fiction novel. However, they aren't science fiction or any other kind of fiction. Computer terms and its language are real, and in spite of appearances, computerese is not as confusing and confounding as a novice might think.

You may already be familiar with computer terms and their meanings. If this is so, please skip this chapter and go directly to chapter 5. On the other hand, if you have heard terms like "byte," "bit," "CPU," or "floppy disk," but aren't too confident of their meanings and relationships, reading this chapter may help you. If you simply don't know any computer terms, then a study of chapter 4 and appendix 1 would be beneficial to understanding computers in general and how they can be used in the church.

Related to chapter 4 and appendix 1 is a computer term glossary provided in appendix 2. This glossary is designed to help you quickly refer to the most common computer terms that you'll need to survive in the world of automation. You may use it to help you later in dealing with vendors when they assume you understand all those technical terms. The glossary may also be helpful if you are going on to chapter 5 and later find a computer term that you do not know. All terms described in the text and found in the glossary are italicized.

The Language of Computers

The language of the computer world does not require any special background or knowledge. It requires, like any other new language you may learn, perseverance in order to develop sufficient mastery that you may productively apply it to the church. The objective of this chapter is to provide you with enough knowledge to start walking the path towards becoming a computerese master. In addition, what you learn should greatly assist you in intelligently communicating with vendors who offer their computer products to the church.

This computerese journey begins by stating what a computer is *not*. A computer is not a brain. Very often computers are popularly referred to as brains, but a brain is capable of emotional responses and learns from its own mistakes. A computer is not capable of producing emotions because it is a machine and therefore does not have a spiritual capacity. In addition, only a very few experimental computers are able to learn. These have been previously described in chapter 2. Brains think and learn, whereas computers are slaves that do exactly what they are told to do.

If a computer is not a brain, then what is it? A computer is a tool. It is a machine that enhances information processing. A more formal definition of a computer might be, "a machine or device composed of logical electronic circuits designed to generate desired output in a specified sequence from a logical set of instructions as produced from a given set of input data." This definition is one of many that exists for computers and might be a computer scientist's laboratory version. What this really means for the church, however, is that the computer is a tool that assists human beings to process information more efficiently.

Consider for a moment a spoon that is used to stir a pot of soup cooking on your stove or a hammer used to drive a nail so that you can hang a picture on your wall. In both of these cases, the spoon and the hammer are tools used for particular purposes. They are "means" whereby you are able to accomplish a desired "end." A computer is a tool that the church can use to assist the management of its information to build a more solid ministry for Christ. Computer technology is the means to achieve the desired end of better ministry information management.

It is very important in all discussions about computers to remember that computers are simply tools for the overall work of God. History has shown that the church frequently allowed new inventions and ideas to become the primary emphasis for the church. In other words, idols have often replaced the simple worship of God and detracted from simple ministry. With the fascination computers have for human beings, it becomes even more important not to let the computer become the church's idol of future decades. Thus, the church must strive to intentionally remind itself that a computer is no more and no less than a tool for ministry.

Any common tool used for any purpose requires a human being to direct it. A tool by itself is an inanimate object that has no life of its own. However, when a human being commands the tool, it becomes part of the person in creating something.

Likewise, the key to understanding a computer is that it must be directed by some person. It is a machine that is directed in a very specific way. Without the direction, the machine becomes a useless object. All it will do is sit and stare. It must be told everything before it can do anything. A computer must be commanded by a living, breathing person to make it a valuable part of the task being attempted.

Software and Computer Languages

In order for a person to command the computer, he or she must communicate specific instructions to the machine. A set of these very specific, person-designed and created instructions for a particular purpose is a computer *program*. A computer program is a logical grouping of very precise instructions that informs the computer exactly what to do and when to do it.

Programming, therefore, is the art or skill of writing a program for the computer. Programming requires specialized knowledge that a church secretary, for example, does *not* need in order to use the computer.

The *programmer*, then, is the human being that does the programming to create a program for a specific purpose. A professional programmer would be employed by a business or nonprofit organization to develop computer programs to meet the needs of that organization. Your church probably will *not* need a programmer on its staff. Rather, a programmer would be utilized through a professional programming firm much like an attorney is often retained to do the church's legal work.

You may also frequently hear the term *software* when discussing computers. Software is a synonym for a computer program. If a person remarks about "writing software," a reference is being made to programming.

A *software package* is a set of two or more programs designed for an overall system with several specific functions. For example, your church might purchase a software package to maintain local church finances. This overall system would probably include specific functions related to the general ledger, pledge accounting, and writing checks.

In order to write software, i.e., to program the computer, the programmer must be familiar with a computer *language*. In-depth communication with a computer requires knowledge of a computer programming language. Every computer has its own language, and many computers may share the same language provided an easy method of exchanging software exists. Software exchange depends on many factors, but for the moment, you should be aware that it is possible to transfer programs from one computer to another in many cases.

There are literally hundreds of computer languages in existence today with almost every language broken into several dialects, depending upon the particular computer you are using. Some of the more common languages are FORTRAN, COBOL, PASCAL, and BASIC. BASIC is the most widely used language in the small computer market today. Most commercially available church software packages are currently written in BASIC. This is because BASIC is an easy language to learn and use on a practical level. It is also a very simple process to modify BASIC programs allowing great adaptability of the software in meeting a church's needs.

If you wish to communicate with your computer on an in-depth level, the burden of knowing and understanding the language is your responsibility. Computer programming, however, is not difficult. It is generally true that anyone can write a very elementary computer program in BASIC after about two hours of instruction. However, patience is vital because it takes time and maturity to become sophisticated in programming.

Your church situation will probably not require the staff to become skilled in programming. You do not need to know a computer programming language in order to use a computer. At some point, however, it may be advantageous for one or more of the church staff to learn and use a computer language. This could help you develop software for the very specific needs within your church.

Hardware

True software in any computer is a nebulous, intangible entity. It can only be utilized through the computer *hardware*.

In other words, the hardware allows the software to function. Computer hardware, quite simply, is the nuts and bolts, the wires and circuits, the buttons you push, and switches you throw. The hardware is what you see demonstrated in a computer store.

In order for a computer to be a computer, both hardware and software are required. As an analogy, a human being is composed of a physical body and a spiritual body. In a computer system, the hardware is analogous to the human physical body and the software is parallel to the human spiritual body. In many ways, the computer is an extension of human powers, i.e., a tool to enhance the wholeness of a human person.

The fundamental hardware required in any computer consists of three items:

1. An *input* device.
2. An *output* device.
3. A *central processing unit* (CPU).

On modern day computers, the input device is usually a keyboard like a typewriter, which allows the operator to enter information into the computer. Each time you touch a key, a signal or code is generated in the computer that represents the key you pressed. That signal is then placed into the computer's memory.

Computers of the 1950s, 1960s, and even some in the 1970s, used the *punched card* as their primary input device. Holes were punched in a stiff paper card through a device called a *keypunch*. A keypunch was a typewriter-like device a fraction smaller than a standard size desk. The holes punched in the card formed patterns that represented letters, numbers, and punctuation. The information on the cards was then entered into the computer via an input device called a *punched card reader*.

The CPU manipulates the information into the desired form, and also controls all other internal functions of the machine. In order for the CPU to do its work, *memory* is required. Units of computer memory are called *bits* and *bytes*.

33

A byte (pronounced "bite") is formed by several bits, and each byte represents a character such as a letter, numeral, punctuation, or the blank space. A thousand bytes is a *K*, and a million bytes is an *MB*. In other words, 64K is equal to 64,000 bytes or characters and 5MB is equal to 5 million bytes or characters. If you feel the need for more information on bits and bytes, please see appendix 1 for a more detailed discussion of this subject.

The CPU's memory is often called *core* memory, which refers to its fundamental function. Other names for core memory frequently used by vendors are *RAM* (Random Access Memory) or *ROM* (Read Only Memory). RAM and ROM each have different functions depending on the manufacturer. Regardless of its type, core memory processes information very rapidly, being able to do literally tens of thousands of complex arithmetic calculations in one second.

The output device prints the information needed into the form requested. The output device could be a screen or a printer.

The screen is like a television screen that visually displays the information you request. The screen output device is frequently called a *VDT* (video display tube) or *CRT* (cathode ray tube). A VDT is usually called a "monitor" by vendors.

A *printer* is like a typewriter without a keyboard. It prints information onto paper. It does this through a mechanism that strikes a ribbon and makes an imprint on the paper. The variety and types of printers are extensive. The most common in the small computer market are *dot matrix* and *letter quality*. A dot matrix printer is relatively fast and is good for printing long reports. A letter quality printer is slower but produces output that looks as if it was typed on a standard typewriter. Actual printing speeds are usually referred to in *cps* (characters per second) or *lpm* (lines per minute).

Some hardware devices provide both input and output functions. Generally, these are the magnetic storage devices such as a cassette tape, *floppy disk* or *hard disk*. These pieces of hardware are sometimes called *mass* storage devices because of their capacity to store very large amounts of information in a very small physical space. Information may be either outputted from or inputted to any mass storage device.

When discussing mass storage devices, usually there is a functional difference between the *drive* and the media. For example, to use a cassette tape, you would use a common cassette tape recorder/player. You may have many tapes, but the recorder/player unit allows you to use all your tapes. From a computer's standpoint, the cassette recorder/player is considered a tape drive. In like manner, the device that records and plays information to or from either floppy or hard disks is called a drive such as a floppy disk drive.

On the other hand, the magnetic media is a special material used on tapes and disks that responds to electronic impulses from the drive. The computer directs the drive to either output information to the tape or disk, or input information from them. A more detailed description of the storage capacities and types of mass storage devices is given in chapter 7.

The least efficient and least expensive mass storage device initially is cassette tape. The most efficient and most expensive initially is the hard disk. The floppy disk is between tape and hard disk in both efficiency and cost. Hard disks, however, are the most cost effective in the long term. A church computer operation *must* have a mass storage device, preferably either floppy or hard disks. Otherwise the church's information cannot be stored for later retrieval and manipulation.

After reading and digesting this chapter, you have taken the first step toward becoming a computerese master. On the other hand, if you don't want to be a computerese master, then you have just enough knowledge to hold a reasonably intelligent conversation about computers with a vendor or friend. In any case, by using your newly found knowledge in contemplating computerized Christendom, the apparently mysterious nature of computerese should become less baffling and more exciting.

Chapter 5

PLANNING FOR A CHURCH COMPUTER: TRYING TO PUT GOD'S GRACE IN A BOX

About seven months after becoming part of the United Methodist General Council on Finance and Administration staff, I was called by the chairperson of a local church administrative board. His first words to me were, "Our church just bought a computer—what are we supposed to do with it?" Since then, numerous other local churches also have bought computers, with the common thread of belief being that all they needed to do was install the computer and it would run itself. Unfortunately, this is not true as many have discovered.

To adequately plan for the installation of a church computer is a great deal like trying to put God's grace in a box. It can't be done. Experience has demonstrated again and again that no matter how many questions one raises and answers about a computer operation, there is something that always seems to be overlooked. In many ways, Murphy's law is quite applicable here: If something can go wrong, it will. Yet, the proposed installation of a church computer must be studied carefully if a balance between efficiency and good stewardship is to be created. If such a balance can be achieved, the computer can assist the church in developing a deeper faithfulness in its ministry.

Prior to the purchase and installation of a computer, significant analysis and in-depth planning must occur. If done correctly, analysis and planning can make the computer an effective tool much more quickly in your church. The primary objective of chapters 5 through 11 is to assist the church with planning for a computer. These chapters are not intended to cover every detail in the analysis and planning process. However, this information can be a guide for the proper study of local church computer needs, and provide a path to a smoother and more effective transition to the computer for the entire congregation.

A Computer Committee

Before beginning to plan for a computer in the church, it is advisable to form a "Computer Committee" or "Computer Study Task Force." Such groups should be composed of five to ten persons from your church, depending upon congregational size. Some of the committee members, if possible, should have professional computer backgrounds, and there should be others who have no technical computer skills. The pastor and church secretary who will more than likely be the primary operators of the computer should be included on the committee as ex officio members. The role of this group should be studying all phases of a computer beginning with the church's computer needs, making recommendations, and supervising the installation and implementation of the computer.

After the committee is formed, the first step in the study process is to educate the group about computers. The members should have computer terms defined, understand the capabilities of computers, and be able to relate those to the church. Learning about computers could occur through reading a book such as this one, having one of the committee members talk about computers, or by inviting a local professional to give a two-hour crash course one evening. The process of computer education could also occur through a combination of these approaches. Whatever learning method is used, computer education is required so that your group may make sound recommendations about a computer for your church.

Needs Analysis

Once the formal computer learning has taken place, your committee is ready to begin its work. The proper place to begin is by assessing the church's ministry and administrative needs. In other words, a "needs analysis" of your church must be completed as the *primary step* for a computer. The purpose of the needs analysis is to clearly identify what information currently is being received by and used in the church, and whether a computer could save time in controlling that data.

The needs analysis should not be restricted to administrative functions. It should encompass all aspects of program ministry including evangelism, social concerns, church school, missions, etc. These areas should be analyzed to determine:

1. What information is needed for their work.
2. How the information is received.
3. How the information is used.
4. How the information is maintained.
5. What forms both the received and used information takes.

The administrative procedures in most churches are manual systems that consume large blocks of time. These systems should be studied to determine how a computer could help those processes. For example, consider the procedure used to address the monthly newsletter or weekly bulletin mailed to church members.

1. Is the church secretary (or pastor) using four-part carbon-type labels that must be retyped every four months?
2. Is the secretary actually writing by hand names and addresses onto the document to be mailed?
3. How much time does the entire process take?
4. A related question is how much time does it take the secretary to manually complete a change of address and update other membership information used in church mailings?

If this is a manual process that occurs in your church, answers to the above questions should lead to the conclusion that a computer could easily automate church mailings. Other areas to examine are finances, membership data records, skills and talents inventory of church members, etc.

The key questions in the needs analysis are: What are you going to do with a computer? What will the computer do that produces a more effective ministry for the church? What are the potential applications of a computer in your church?

Potential Computer Applications

Historically, the need for computers in the church has been generated by the desire for better financial control and more accurate fiscal information. However, computer potential in the local church goes far beyond this in terms of overall ministry. This is illustrated in Table 5-1, which contains a listing of possible computer applications in a local church. This list is by no means exhaustive. It is provided as an idea generator for the church's study. Hopefully, it can help to produce additional applications that lend themselves to automation within your particular situation.

TABLE 5-1

POTENTIAL COMPUTER
APPLICATIONS IN THE LOCAL CHURCH

1. Membership records of individuals and families that may include names, addresses, birthdays, calling zones, offices held, skills and talents inventory, etc.
2. Membership changes including new members added, transfers, members removed by church board action, etc.
3. Records of deaths, marriages, and baptisms.
4. Pledge accounting.

5. General ledger bookkeeping; receipts and disbursements; automatic check writing.
6. Payroll.
7. Facilities management including energy controls, reception booking and planning, inventory of office supplies, general inventory, etc.
8. Statistical information about worship attendance, church school attendance, the number of baptisms during the year, etc.
9. Mailing lists and labels.
10. Planning and research analysis of membership patterns, likes and dislikes, etc.
11. Listings of board, council, and committee members.
12. Inventory of Christian education materials.
13. Records of church school attendance, offerings, members, teachers, etc.
14. Direct teaching in the church school using computer assisted instruction with tutorials, drill and practice, and simulation (role playing).
15. Letter and document production through word processing techniques (including church newsletters and bulletins).
16. Worship attendance records identifying persons who regularly miss worship, or who have missed three or more Sundays after faithful attendance.
17. Pastoral call and visitation records.
18. Records of hymns used, prayers used, Scripture used, and other items used in worship.
19. Sermon records including sermon title, Scripture, associated hymns, topic, "one" sentence description, where preached, date preached, appropriate liturgical season, etc.
20. Children's sermon records.
21. Electronic mail between churches and judicatory offices.

22. Equipment depreciation and servicing records, history of insurance values and agents.
23. Generation of judicatory reporting forms.
24. Biblical concordance and research.

Some Concrete Examples

To help crystallize your church's unique situation, below are two different examples of how a computer can be used in the church.

1. **Birthday remembrance.**
   - Many pastors like to remember the birthdays of church members within the congregation. This is a simple personal gesture that the pastor can use to maintain contact with church members during the year.
   - Under a manual system, one must go into the files, pull out sheets of paper for particular days or months, and have them listed by the secretary (or by the pastor if no secretary exists!). Of course, some provision must be made to add new members' birthdays and delete the birthdays of members who have left the congregation during the previous year. From this list, an appropriate response such as a birthday card, a telephone call, letter, or pastoral visit can be made.
   - This manual process can consume from ten minutes to one hour depending upon the church's size and how well organized the files are in the first place. It can also be very cumbersome, reducing the pastor's time for people because the administration of this simple task is a burden.
   - If the birthday information was loaded into the church computer, it would be a very easy task for the pastor to request a list of all persons with birthdays in a particular month, week, or even on a certain day. The list would be automatically generated with addresses, telephone numbers, calling zones, and other pertinent

information useful to the pastor. The automated process requires less than one minute of the pastor's or secretary's time and about five minutes for the computer to print the information, depending upon the printer's speed.

2. **Ministry to the bereaved.**
   - Frequently the first anniversary of a loved one's death can be an emotional strain for the spouse and family. Some pastors have the habit of noting the first anniversary of a church member's death a year in advance on their calendar. The notation then serves as a timely reminder to initiate a pastoral response. This may not be a time-consuming task except when the new year arrives and all those dates must be transferred to the pastor's new calendar.
   - By keeping records of church members' deaths in the church computer, a list can be generated on a monthly, weekly, or even daily basis of all persons who had died the previous year at that particular time. This list can save time for the pastor who can make a pastoral call at this crucial period.

Using the computer in both of these instances provides a significant savings in time for the pastor and secretary. The process of noting information on a calendar or filing it away and then having to search for it later on a periodic basis is tedious and time consuming. The computer can easily maintain and remember this data, producing an important enhancement to the work of ministry. It allows the pastor and parish workers a deeper awareness of problems and stressful events in the lives of church members so that appropriate pastoral responses can be made.

These examples may have caused you to think of areas in your own church and ministry where a computer can provide remarkable assistance. You may discover after doing a needs analysis that your church can't justify a computer, and that's fine. The church should obviously continue with its manual systems. On the other hand, you may find many items that would allow the pastor and parish workers to be freed from the mundane tasks of administration to respond to the human needs and ministry of your church.

In summary, the purpose of the needs analysis is to determine what manual systems can be automated *and* how much time would be saved in those tasks. The result should be growth in the church's ministry and life as a community of faith. It is best not to begin planning for a church computer by going to a local computer store and viewing their wares. Always begin by deciding what you would do with a computer in your church and whether those applications justify a computer. After the needs analysis is completed, with identified benefits justifying a computer for your church, continue with the rest of the study.

Chapter 6

FINDING THE
RIGHT SPIRITUAL SOFTWARE

The software of any computer is, in essence, its spirit. It is the software that provides the computer with its "personality" and allows it to be a functional tool for the church. After completing the needs analysis and stating the benefits of a computer for your church, your computer committee can define a software configuration. This configuration will become the specifications and requirements for a complete computer software system that meets the church's needs. This chapter will discuss the evaluation and selection of the software for a complete church computer system.

It is extremely important that the software be chosen before the hardware. **NEVER, NEVER CHOOSE THE HARD-WARE BEFORE THE SOFTWARE.** The hardware is really incidental to the software because the software meets the church's needs much more than the hardware. However, if the hardware is selected first, your software choices probably will be limited and will not come anywhere close to meeting the church's defined needs.

There are two questions your committee should discuss concerning software. The first question concerns what software is available from where. The second question concerns evaluation as various software packages are considered and rated.

Software Availability

Numerous computer vendors and software houses are marketing a variety of local church software packages. The competition among the vendors is quite fierce as each attempts to offer software from financial applications to membership control to word processing to church school programs. However, most of the available software for churches concentrates upon church financial and membership data control. Many vendors also offer *turnkey* computer systems. A turnkey system is a combination of hardware and software usually sold at special discount rates.

To determine who the vendors are, you may wish to write or call church judicatory offices. Several denominations have compiled local church software vendor lists for distribution upon request. By writing state, regional, and/or national church offices, the study committee may be able to obtain such a list to begin the search for appropriate software.

Your church can also ask neighboring churches if they are aware of any local church computer software. Asking other churches could be a good source of information. In addition, many computer stores may be able to lead you in the direction of local church software. However, bear in mind that their own self-interests may prevail in their advice to the church.

Software Evaluation

The other major area of church software needing thoughtful analysis is evaluation. Before selecting the software, the committee needs to know how the software works and precisely what it is designed to do. The following are areas to analyze in software evaluation:

1. **Relation to needs analysis.**
   - An examination of potential software packages should be completed using the church's original needs analysis as a foundation. The purpose of this is to determine if the software will meet the congregation's needs. For example, your needs analysis may indicate you want to maintain the name, address, birthday information, date of baptism, date of confirmation, date of transfer,

and past and present committee memberships for each church member. A thorough review of the software will enable the committee to decide if the package will maintain this sort of information.

- In most instances, the software may not exactly conform to the needs analysis. The decision about software really revolves around which package comes the closest to meeting the congregation's needs without modifying the church's overall information system.

2. **User friendly.**

- A second area of software evaluation concerns its user friendliness. A *user friendly* software package means that it is easy to use from the operator's view. The committee should examine how easy the software is to use from the operator's vantage point. A user friendly software system will have a HELP command that can be used at any time. The information printed when the help command is entered should inform the operator what the next step is supposed to be. Also, a user friendly system will have easy-to-understand *prompts* and questions as the software works. For example, instead of "C?" a user friendly system would print "please enter command." Complete phrases to assist the operator are a sign that the software is user friendly. (A prompt is basically a question printed on the screen that requires the operator to enter a response before the program continues.)

- As the committee begins to evaluate software systems, it will discover that many systems are not user friendly. In fact, a large amount of commercially available software can be quite difficult to use. This is because software is often written from a programmer's point of view rather than from a church secretary's need. In other words, they are "user belligerent." Therefore, user friendliness should be carefully scrutinized because it will determine in a large measure how easily your church computer operation becomes a reality.

3. **Software interfaces.**
   • Linkage of the software from application to application is another evaluative concern. This linkage from one computer program to another is called software *interface*. Interface is generally a matter of degrees and refers to how well and how easily programs written for different purposes access common data files. The interface question is important for the church because it reduces duplication of effort. The following examples will help clarify this linkage.
      a. How are the pledge accounting and general ledger systems interfaced? Will the pledge accounting system that maintains the contributions of church members automatically total a particular Sunday's offering and credit the proper general ledger account?
      b. Does the membership data base link with the pledge accounting system? This would be important so that information in the pledge accounting system and the membership data base needs to be entered only once. For example, a change of address should be entered only once for both systems.
   • The type of linkage described in the above examples illustrates the importance of properly interfaced software. The data required by each church computer need should be analyzed to see where commonality of information exists. This analysis will provide the committee with a relative view of potential software efficiency and the amount of duplicated effort that will be required. Software interfaces are necessary to make a computer system fully functional for the church. Without them, you could spend as much time in duplicated effort as you used for the manual systems the computer replaced!

- Vendors often use the word *integration* in place of *interface;* however, software integration is a buzzword that sounds good in a sales pitch and is greatly overused. When a vendor uses the word *integration*, you should ask him or her to identify precisely the interfaces the software uses.

4. **Other churches that use the software.**
   - Ask the vendor to provide you with a list of churches that are already using their software. The study committee can then contact these other churches and inquire about their level of satisfaction with the package being investigated. You should determine if the software meets their needs and whether or not it works for them.

5. **Documentation.**
   - The committee should carefully review the documentation that comes with the software system. Understandable and complete documentation (user manuals) is a major key to the effective utilization of a computer. Does the documentation seem to be comprehensive, covering various contingencies and problems? The documentation should assist the user in following the software prompts and *menus* on the screen with descriptive information about what the prompt means and the proper information to be entered. (A menu is a list of items presented on the screen from which the operator chooses an application to be run.) Are the manuals easy to use and read? Terms must be clearly and precisely stated so that they make sense to you. The church's designated computer operator also should examine the documentation and give his/her opinion about it. For example, if the secretary will be the chief operator, he/she should tell the study committee if the documentaion is readable, easy to use, and helpful. For the most part, it is this person who must use the

computer on a daily basis, and therefore, the documentation should be readable to him/her.

6. **Software demonstration.**
   • Ask the software vendor to provide a demonstration of their software. If they are truly interested in selling their software, they will make every effort to oblige. A practical demonstration of the proposed software will show you whether the software can fulfill the church's informational needs.

7. **Long-term support.**
   • Another significant area to evaluate is what long-term software support is provided by the vendor. What happens if an error occurs in the program and you don't know what to do or how to correct it? Who will answer your questions? Or, suppose that after a period of time you decide a particular item in the software needs to be modified to fit the church's changing needs. Who will change it? If the change is made by someone other than the vendor, will it void any future support from the vendor? Some vendors offer free support and others charge a per hour cost. Some vendors provide free software support for six months or a year, and then institute a charge after the grace period has expired. In any case, it is crucial to know what long-term software support is available and how much it will cost to adequately plan and prepare for a church computer.

8. **Training.**
   • To effectively use any software, training is generally required. Some vendors offer initial training periods with the purchase or lease of software. Others don't offer formal training, but give you self-instructional manuals. Unbelievably, some vendors don't offer any training or help and expect you to learn it all on your own.
   • The training may also cost money. Some vendors provide two hours or two days free training with the

purchase or lease of their software package. Any training required beyond the initial free time will be charged at a per hour or per day cost. Other vendors charge extra for their training from the very first minute. In any case, you should be aware of these charges so that unexpected costs are less likely to occur.

• Also, it is good to know where the training is actually held. Sometimes, a vendor staff person will come to the church and provide the training. On the other hand, you and/or the church's staff may have to travel to the vendor's location. If your church is in Colorado and you buy software from a vendor in New York that only offers training in their office, substantial travel costs are involved. In this case, however, you may decide the training and the software are not worth it.

To further assist you, a list of questions and comments is presented below to help you evaluate and select the most appropriate software for your church:

1. **Needs analysis.**
   a. Does the software meet the church's information needs?
   b. Does it fit your input or source documents, i.e., do you have to rewrite the information before entering it into the computer?
   c. Can you output the church's information in a form acceptable to the various church groups that will use the computer?
   d. Does the data maintained by the software match the church's data needs list?

2. **User friendly.**
   a. Is the software user friendly in the opinion of your operator?
   b. Is it easy to use and understandable?
   c. Does it have a HELP option that provides the operator with assistance in getting out of a problem or answering a question?

3. **Linkage or interface.**
   a. How are the various software functions interfaced?
   b. Is duplication of effort eliminated because an address change is made only once that updates all necessary computer files?
4. **Other churches that use it.**
   a. Obtain a list of other churches using the software.
   b. Contact them to determine their satisfaction with the system.
   c. Does the software meet their needs?
   d. Does it work properly?
   e. Have they had any problems in using it? If so, what were the difficulties? How were the problems resolved, and what did the vendor do to help?
   f. Do they feel the software is user friendly?
   g. Has the vendor been supportive?
5. **Documentation.**
   a. Does the vendor have adequate documentation (manuals, etc.) to support the software? Ask to see it.
   b. Is the documentation complete and comprehensive?
   c. Does it provide a blow-by-blow description of the software prompts and menus?
   d. Carefully review the documentation to determine if you understand it.
   e. Is the documentation written in terms that any person *without* computer knowledge can understand?
   f. Does it include descriptions of errors that the software may generate? If an error occurs, does the user's manual suggest a way to correct the error?
6. **Demonstration.**
   a. Ask the vendor for a demonstration of the software.
   b. Does it seem to work?
   c. Will it really meet your needs?
7. **Long-term support.**
   a. If a software error occurs, who provides support?
   b. Who will correct the error?

c. If the vendor doesn't correct the error and refers you to another software house or independent contractor, then:
   1. Who is this third party?
   2. What are their qualifications?
   3. How responsive and reliable are they in correcting errors?
d. After the software has been installed, who specifically answers questions that may arise?
e. Is there a telephone number that the church may call to receive the necessary information?
f. Is there a project manager assigned by the vendor to answer questions if it is not explained in the documentation?
g. What guarantees can the vendor offer that the software will not be *down* for more than one week if an error develops? ("Down" is a computerese term that simply means the computer doesn't work.) Note that one week is an arbitrary figure that may be applicable in some church situations and not to others. Your church must decide how long it could do without the computer due to a software problem. This period may be one day, one week, or one month.
h. Software modification.
   1. Will the vendor modify the software for the church's particular needs?
   2. If so, will they support the modification over the next five to ten years?
   3. What does such a modification cost?
   4. Under what conditions can a church member or another software house modify the vendor's software?
   5. If someone other than the vendor modifies the software, is any previous vendor support agreement voided? Are there any penalties?
i. New software releases by the vendor.

1. If the vendor produces new releases of the software, will the church receive them automatically?
2. What is the projected cost of new software releases?
3. If any conversion is necessary to use the new software releases, will the vendor assist in the conversion process? (Conversion is a method whereby the new software release must be slightly changed to function on your computer. Not all new software releases from your original vendor will work on the computer the vendor advised you to buy. Thus, a conversion process is required.)

8. **Training.**
   a. Who provides training in using the software?
   b. Does the vendor offer free training up to a certain limit when you purchase the software?
   c. If more training is required than the initial free instruction:
      1. How much does it cost?
      2. Where will the training occur? In the church or at the vendor's office?
   d. Is the training self-instructional, i.e., a method whereby the church staff learns to use the software through a programmed instruction manual?
   e. What training is offered with future software releases, and what is the projected cost?

From the point of wholeness, it is important to carefully evaluate how the software will affect you and the congregation. You are the ones that must live with it on a long-term basis. You must make it work for an improvement of ministry within your church. One of the keys to using a computer and its software is that it should fit your needs rather than you having to fit the computer's needs. In other words, the computer should work for you as a tool. You shouldn't be working for it. The *only adequate* way to insure this is a careful analysis that results in your selecting only the most appropriate software for your church.

Chapter 7

TO BE OR NOT
TO BE: FINDING A LEAN,
MEAN, COMPUTING MACHINE

After the study committee has settled on appropriate software for the church, the time has arrived to evaluate and select hardware. Finding a lean, mean, computing machine that is right for the church may appear to be a formidable task. However, because the study committee has chosen the software first, hardware evaluation and selection follow a natural course. This is because only one or two types of hardware will probably be able to support the software the church has chosen. On the other hand, when the software chosen is based on one of the mainline *operating systems* (CP/M, CP/M-86, MS-DOS, Unix) it will operate on several brands of hardware. This requires an evaluation and selection process to determine which computer has the greatest potential of meeting the church's needs. (An operating system is a software package that oversees the entire work of a computer. Please see appendix 1 for a more detailed discussion of operating systems.)

Frequently your software vendor will recommend a particular brand of hardware. Such a recommendation can prove beneficial because it practically eliminates the need to compare and evaluate two or more machines. However, it is best to not accept blindly the vendor's hardware suggestions. Rather, the committee should evaluate the vendor's recommended computers using the factors described in the following paragraphs. The results of this analysis will help build your confidence in the vendor or cause you to reject your original software selection and begin the process again.

Hardware Options

If the church is faced with the problem of choosing a certain brand of hardware from two or more machines, the basic key is to select the one that most adequately fits your needs. As with software, the church must live with its decision about hardware. In the long term, a proper hardware choice will contribute to a useful church management information system becoming a reality more quickly. The following areas should be considered in your hardware examination:

1. **Processor (CPU) bit size.**
   - The bit size of the processor refers to the number of bits and bytes that can be manipulated at any given moment. The larger the bit size, the more efficient and fast the hardware.
   - In the microcomputer world, the common bit sizes are 8, 16, and 32. The microcomputers that were first sold in the marketplace used 8-bit processors. The 8-bit machines can be considered the first generation of microcomputers. Most microcomputers available from vendors today are the 16 or 32 bit variety.
   - Generally, computer operating systems are tied to the bit size of the processor. Table 7-1 shows these relationships.

TABLE 7-1

PROCESSOR BIT SIZE AND OPERATING SYSTEMS

Bit Size	Operating Systems
8	CP/M
16	CP/M-86, MS-DOS, Unix
32	CP/M-86, MS-DOS, Unix

   - If your church wants to take advantage of new software trends, it is advisable to examine only the 16- or 32-bit computers. Purchasing the larger bit size will provide

the church with state-of-the-art technology. On the
other hand, as the larger bit machines become more
prevalent, many good used 8-bit computers will be for
sale. This means your church may be able to purchase
an older, but perfectly adequate computer for its
purposes. Generally, used microcomputers can be
obtained inexpensively; however, the committee
should evaluate a used computer as thoroughly as a new
one.

2. **Television monitor or video display tube (VDT).**
 • VDTs come in all sizes, shapes, and colors. Frequently,
   the VDT will be limited to a particular model specified
   by the vendor. However, you may also be given a
   number of choices in VDTs:

   Color (Usually the most expensive, but most dramatic
       and helpful with graphic displays such as bar
       graphs, pie charts, and other visual effects.)
   Black and White (Adequate for church use; when
       compared to color, it is less expensive and less
       complicated.)
   Amber and White (Similar to black and white; costs
       more than black and white but less than color;
       easiest on the eyes according to studies.)
   Green and White (Similar to black and white; costs
       about the same as black and white.)

 • After determining the available VDT options on the
   computers being examined, persons who will be using
   the computer the greatest amount should view each of
   the monitors. Then they should be asked for their
   preferences. This will assist the study committee in
   choosing the best monitor for the church while being
   sensitive to those who will be using it the most.

3. **Special function keys for word processing.**
 • Some hardware keyboards provide special keys to
   make word processing much easier. For example,
   cursor movement keys considerably reduce the time

necessary for editing a document. Other keys might include "center," "line," "page," "search and replace," etc. If the church plans on doing large amounts of word processing, these special functions are important to efficient computer utilization. Computers without such keys tend to increase the time required for document creation and editing.

- Some computers also require an "80-column board" to do word processing. This is a circuit board that produces 80 columns on the screen instead of 40, which is common to many microcomputers. An 80-column screen is essential for efficient and beneficial word processing. Without it, the operator can see only one-half of a line, which would be very inconvenient. The hardware vendor will tell you if an 80-column board is required for the word processing software on the computers you are evaluating.

4. **Floppy disks and disk drives.**

- For the most efficient system use, at least two floppy disk drives should be purchased with the computer. In addition, the church should plan to have about 2K (2,000 bytes) of total storage for every church member. For example, if your church has five hundred members, 1,000K (or 1 MB) of storage will be needed. If the church has two thousand members, 4,000K (or 4 MB) of storage is needed. This guideline is not meant to apply in every church situation. However, it should help you get started and allow some room for growth.

- Also, the following factors about floppy disks should be reviewed:

  a. **Physical disk size.**

  - The size of disks can be 8, 5¼, and 3½ inches. The most popular and common are 5¼" disks. The 8" disk is an older style, and the 3½" is a new technology that has not yet won wide acceptance.

b. **Sides and density.**

- Floppy disks come with two physical sides. However, disks also come with one or two logical sides. For instance, a disk *drive* may have read/write heads for only one side of the disk. When this is true, floppy disks with only one logical side must be used. A floppy disk with only one logical side is called a *single-side* disk. If the disk drive has read/write heads that can physically access both sides of the floppy, then the floppy disks that can be used in that drive are called *dual-side* or double side. This means the disk has two logical sides as well as two physical sides.

- The density of a floppy disk refers to how information is stored on the disk. As a disk becomes more dense, it can store more information. There are numerous levels of floppy disk density. The most common in today's microcomputers include *single density* and *double density*. Higher density disks are available, but are usually limited to specific computers not necessarily applicable to the work of the church.

- For church and home use, floppy disks come with four possible combinations of sides and density. These are:
    1. Single side, single density (SS/SD)
    2. Dual side, single density (DS/SD)
    3. Single side, dual density (SS/DD)
    4. Dual side, dual density (DS/DD)

- The single-side, single-density disks have the least amount of potential storage in a physical area. The dual-side, dual-density disks have the greatest amount of storage in the same physical space. Options 2 and 3 are in between the other two. In order to have as much data *on line* at any one time, the best choice in sides and density is number 4.

(On line refers to information available at any one moment without needing to load a different disk.) Generally, two SS/SD floppies give about 320K of on-line storage and two DS/DD floppies give about 1.2 MB of on-line storage. The hardware determines the combination of sides and density required. If possible, the church should seek a computer with DS/DD capability for the sake of efficiency and cost effectiveness.

5. **Hard disks.**

- If you need more data on line than is offered through floppy disks, a hard disk may be a better option for the church. Hard disks can hold between five and twenty times more data on line than two dual-side, dual-density floppy disks. Hard disks are also much faster than floppies, *and* the cost per character (byte) is much less than floppy disks. However, their initial cost is greater. Table 7-2 gives a comparison of initial and per byte costs of these mass storage devices. The initial costs are shown estimates that will decrease proportionately as new less expensive hardware is introduced. Examination of the table demonstrates that the cost of mass storage decreases as the size of the disk increases.

TABLE 7-2

CENTS/BYTE FOR MASS STORAGE

Type	Total Storage	Initial Cost	Cost/byte
Floppy (DS/DD)	1.2MB	$2,500	$0.002083
Hard	5.0MB	$5,000	$0.001
Hard	10.0MB	$6,000	$0.0006
Hard	20.0MB	$7,500	$0.000375

- If your church can justify the purchase of a hard disk, you should also purchase one floppy disk drive or tape drive for *back-up* purposes (see chapter 9). Unlike the floppy disks that are removable from the drives, a hard disk is usually fixed. This means it is encased in a metal box and cannot be opened except by a qualified technician. Thus, you must have the floppy disk drive in order to make copies (back-ups) of the church's data and software.

6. **Printers.**

• *Printers* come in a variety of sizes and printing speeds for both general and specific purposes. For church computer work, either a *letter quality* or *dot matrix* printer is sufficient.

• A letter quality printer prints information onto paper so that it appears as if you typed on your typewriter. Letter quality printers usually have a "daisy wheel" or similar device that is pushed by a hammer against a ribbon to print a character. Most letter quality printers offer both ten (pica) and twelve (elite) pitch, and some have six, ten, twelve, fifteen, and eighteen pitches. Others provide proportional spacing together with a variety of pitches. For professional looking word processing, a letter quality printer is the better choice. However, to have letter quality output, speed must be sacrificed. Letter quality printers are generally much slower than the dot matrix type and usually have speeds in the 7 characters per second (cps) to 45 *cps* range. Also, letter quality printers can use a forms tractor so regular computer paper and labels can be used. In this way, the church could print reports and labels in letter quality format. If the church purchases a cut sheet feeder, regular typing paper or stationery can be automatically passed through the printer eliminating the need to handle each sheet of paper individually. Without a cut sheet feeder, the operator must place each sheet of paper into the printer and then remove it after the printing has been completed. This type of printer is more expensive than the dot matrix, with prices in the $1,500 to $5,000 range depending on special features and speeds.

• A dot matrix printer is a good printer for printing reports and even some word processing documents. Some dot matrix printers come very close to letter quality printing, but close examination reveals that this type of printing is not true letter quality. Dot matrix printers use *pixels* or very small dots that form in combinations to create the letters. The pixels selected for a particular letter are pressed against a ribbon, which then forms the character on the page. The operator does not need to know which pixels to select. The printer does this through a very special purpose microprocessor built into the device. If your church is not interested in receiving letter quality output, then this type of printer is the better choice. Dot matrix printer speeds usually fall in the range of 30 to 120 cps. Prices of these printers are generally between $500 and $3,000, depending upon features and speed.

• Some vendors offer printers that combine dot matrix and letter quality printing. Such printers serve a dual function by providing fast output for reports and labels while giving the slower letter quality when desired. Speeds of these printers are usually between 15 cps and 80 cps depending upon which mode you are using. Prices range between $1,750 and $3,500.

7. **Communications.**
   • If you want to communicate with other computers, electronic data bases, and/or news services, the church will need to purchase a communications circuit board for the computer. Some computers come with communication features built in and others make it optional equipment.
   • There are two basic types of data communication to consider:

a. **Terminal emulation.**

This type allows your computer to act like a terminal into another computer. It gives you access to the large commercial data bases and electronic mail systems. Most terminal emulation is in ASCII code; however, a few are in EBCDIC. The church should determine the code required by the devices it wants to communicate with before purchasing this option. (See appendix 1 for explanation of ASCII and EBCDIC.)

b. **Protocol.**

This type allows your computer to "talk" directly with other computers. The communication is on a computer-to-computer basis, so that you may transfer files of information between the computers. The two computers that are communicating must have matching protocols in order to talk. A great many protocols exist, but some standardization has occurred. Two of the more standardized protocols are X.25 and the IBM 3780/2780. The computer vendor should be able to assist you with establishing the proper protocol information between computers. If the vendor can't help you, some research into the computer's documentation should shed some light on this mysterious area. If that fails, a letter or telephone call to the manufacturer will be necessary to determine the protocol.

• Some microcomputers will allow both the terminal emulation and protocol boards to be in the computer at the same time. Others will not. In a very few machines, the same circuit board controls both types. The study committee should decide if communicating is important and install either or both of the boards as required. In addition, a software package may have to be purchased to use the communications capability of your computer. The software and hardware board work together to set up the communications. Also a hardware device called a *modem* is required at each end of the communications link (see appendix 1 for a detailed description of modems).

8. **Hardware interfaces.**
   • The simplest hardware interface is a cable that goes between two pieces of computer hardware with standard conventions on the signals carried over the wires. Some more sophisticated interfaces consist of a circuit board installed in the computer. There are two types:

   a. **Serial, usually designated by RS-232C.**
      This interface is very common in the microcomputer market. Almost all modems, printers, monitors, and other devices will be labeled as RS-232C compatible. This informs you that an RS-232C serial interface (cable) is required to electronically connect it to another device. An RS-232C interface has twenty-five wires in the cable, with each wire used for a different signal. Most applications use only six of the wires, but in a few selected cases, all twenty-five wires are used.

   b. **Parallel.**
      These types of interfaces usually refer to printers, although they are not limited to them. Many printers will have both serial and parallel interfaces so that they are compatible with several different computers. If your computer supports only a parallel printer interface, then you will have to purchase a parallel dot matrix or letter quality printer. Most parallel interfaces have thirty-six wires in the cable, with each wire used for a different signal.

Other Hardware Factors

Selecting the proper hardware for your church includes other considerations beyond the types of devices described above. When choosing the hardware, the study committee should become familiar with the following:

1. **Service.**

    Maintenance or service is an important facet of any hardware the church purchases. Just like a copy machine or typewriter, computer hardware occasionally breaks down. When this occurs, a service technician is required to correct the problem. There are two general types of computer servicing systems available.

    a. **On-site.**
    - On-site maintenance means that a repair technician actually comes to the church to fix the computer. You can obtain this type of service by either:

       1. **Buying a maintenance contract.**
           - If you buy a maintenance contract, the church pays a monthly fee much like an insurance premium. This fee entitles the church to on-site service during specified hours of the day. Many maintenance contracts also make limited guarantees about how quickly a technician will be in the church after your telephone call arrives. Materials and parts needed in a service call are usually included within the cost of the maintenance contract. Costs for a maintenance contract generally fall between 1 percent to 2 percent per month of the original computer cost. In other words, if the church pays $5,000 for the hardware, a maintenance contract will cost between $50 and $100 per month.

       2. **Paying time and materials.**
           - If the church pays time and materials, an hourly fee plus the cost of parts and other materials required for the computer is charged. In other words, if a major problem occurs, you may end up replacing almost the entire computer and paying for the cost of all new parts plus the labor to

install it. Also, the church will be charged for the technician's time to travel to and from the church building, plus mileage. Thus, if it takes two hours one way for the technician to travel to and from the building, the church pays an additional four hours labor charge beyond the time required to fix the computer plus mileage. Costs for this type of service are between $50 and $200 per hour depending on the computer and your location. Table 7-3 gives an example of this.

TABLE 7-3

EXAMPLE OF COMPUTER REPAIR ON TIME AND MATERIALS

Standard Labor Charge:	$ 100/hour	
Standard Mileage Charge:	$0.50/mile	
Round Trip Miles	150	$ 75
Total Travel Time	3.0 hours	300
Labor Time at Site	2.0 hours	200
Parts	2 circuit boards	35
Total Charges		$ 610

b. **Depot.**
  - This type of service means that *you* carry the computer in to your computer store if it has a problem. They will either repair it in the store or ship it to a designated repair facility. Charges are based on time and materials plus shipping costs if any. In rare instances a "loaner" computer will be provided, but in most cases the church will simply have to wait until the computer is repaired. The length of time for depot service varies widely and could take one day or six weeks. If your vendor can guarantee repairs in four to six weeks, then the

study committee needs to decide if the church can be without a computer for that length of time. If the church can't be without a computer for that time period, then go to another vendor that offers better service guarantees.

Chapter 8 has additional information on hardware maintenance.

2. **Environment.**

Some computers require special environments to operate. Generally most microcomputers need only a normal office environment. However, "normal" means certain limitations in temperature, humidity, and electricity. These parameters must be followed or damage to the hardware will probably occur. Please see chapter 10 for detailed information on hardware environments and their potential implications for your church.

3. **Expansion potential.**

As your church's understanding of the computer increases, so will your dependence upon the machine. Many new ideas will evolve over time if the church is properly using the computer in a sound ministry management information system. As these new applications are developed on the computer, the day will eventually come when the original computer is not capable of additional tasks. Therefore, the church will either have to buy a new computer or expand; the present one. It is generally less expensive to expand; however, this depends entirely upon your situation. Thus, the study committee should determine if the computers being considered have expansion potential and what that potential is. For example, could a hard disk be added at a later time? Could the RAM storage be increased to accommodate larger, more sophisticated programs? This information will assist in the long range planning for the church's computer operation.

4. Reliability.

To discover whether the computer being evaluated is reliable, the study committee may wish to communicate with other churches and businesses using the same kind of machine. They can tell you if they are satisfied with the hardware and its available support. Usually the vendor can provide a reference list of others for checking purposes. If the vendor isn't willing to do this, then it is probably wise for the study committee to examine other hardware alternatives from other vendors.

5. Documentation.

The study committee should review all relevant manuals and other written materials about the hardware. Like software documentation, is it easy to read? Is the hardware documentation self-explanatory? Is it helpful or is it a hindrance? How is the documentation maintained? These are some questions you may wish to review as the committee studies available documentation.

6. Vendor stability.

Many vendors in the small computer market are here today and gone tomorrow. Thus, it may be wise for the study committee to know how stable the proposed vendor may be. Ask to see a financial statement or annual report of the vendor. Analyze it to see if the company seems to be competent and solvent. Show the financial statement to the church's banker or accountant to receive their objective opinions about the fiscal state of the vendor. Such an analysis may prevent your church from becoming a "computer orphan."

In general, hardware evaluation is both a subjective and objective process. Hardware evaluation is somewhat subjective in qualitative questions concerning reliability, vendor stability, and documentation. It is objective in questions about disk sizes, processor bit size, and printer options. Some authors recommend an evaluation methodology that uses complex statistical weighting processes. Others use a straight one-to-ten rating system on each item and then average the results. All of these methodologies are good, and no one is necessarily better than another. If the study committee feels such a method for evaluating hardware would be helpful, consult some books in your local library or at your local computer store.

Whatever method you use to evaluate hardware, the basic question is if it fulfills the church's defined needs and will operate the selected software. It is the church and no one else that must live with its computer hardware for several years. Therefore, careful analysis is needed to select the best possible computer system for your church and its ministry.

Chapter 8

THE ULTIMATE QUESTION: WHAT DOES IT COST?

One of the most significant factors in purchasing a church computer is the dollar cost. Christians of all communions are cost conscious, desiring the best possible use of available church funds. This historical and often considered sacred task is not easy, requiring great care and integrity. Stewardship of the church's money is a serious concern. Even though stewardship doesn't always mean "cheapest," it does demand that Christians use their funds in the most effective way for the Lord's work.

Choosing the proper computer system for your church is part of good stewardship methodology. The needs analysis will provide the true justification for a computer in the church. Results of the needs analysis will demonstrate savings potential in both time and money. However, church equipment decisions usually are based on cost. Nevertheless, a church computer will have such a significant impact upon the church's ministry that the dollar cost is not the most important issue. Those who make the decision to purchase a church computer should consider the information needs first, and the dollar cost second. Thus, the study committee should be careful not to reduce the decision to "Can we afford it?" The time saved through automating manual systems will show you just how affordable the computer can be for your church. On the other hand, a computer's razzle and dazzle can overwhelm the average person. It is easy to become so fascinated by what a computer can do, that proper cost consideration may be diminished or lost altogether. In other words, the study committee must walk a tightrope between two opposing points of view—affordability versus fascination.

There are two general areas of cost the committee will want to consider in planning for a church computer. They are:

1. Initial, i.e., all funds expended for the initial purchase. This would include the costs of hardware, software, training, physical environment (see chapter 10), materials, etc.
2. Long-term, i.e., the on-going operating costs to maintain a church computer.

These costs will vary from church to church, depending upon the results of the needs analysis and how the computer is ultimately used. However, all congregations using computers will want to budget for these items through regular church planning processes.

Initial Cost

The initial cost of a computer system can be misleading to the unwary. In many ways, buying a computer is similar to buying a car. Buyers begin with the base price, and then add the options that will make the machine suit their needs. Advertisements frequently announce low computer prices with blazing print and fantastic graphics meant to catch your eye. When a vendor indicates that a particular computer sells for $99.95, $595, or $1,795, the figures generally do not include devices that make a computer functional for church information uses.

For example, a well-known manufacturer of microcomputers, Hot-Shot Computer Emporium, Inc., might sell its 64K computer for $795. In their advertising, price comparisons of the Hot-Shot "Love 'Em and Leave 'Em" Model XYZ-007 computer are made with similarly configured computers offered by other vendors. However, what the Hot-Shot ads don't mention is that the $795 includes only the processor (CPU), core memory, and keyboard. This may be sufficient for a home computer, but not for the church.

In order to make the "Love 'Em and Leave 'Em" XYZ-007 computer functional for church work or business needs, the following are needed:

1. A mass storage device such as a floppy disk drive(s), hard disk drive, or a cassette tape drive.
2. A television monitor.
3. A printer.
4. Communication devices for electronic mail and access to large data bases (optional).

After adding items 1, 2, and 3 above to the original cost, that $795 has suddenly become almost $2,500! If you add the communication devices, the cost would probably fall between $2,800 and $3,200. Additionally, the cost for the above Hot-Shot "Love 'Em and Leave 'Em" Model XYZ-007 computer does *not* include any of the initial software, start-up materials (floppy disks, paper, etc.), training (if extra), and environmental factors. Examples of just the software cost include:

Spreadsheet (Visi-Calc, Super-Calc, Multiplan, etc.)	$100 -	$500
Word Processing	$100 -	$1,000
Financial	$100 -	$5,000
Local Church Software	$500 -	$15,000

The above fictitious example based on a real-life computer illustrates that the advertised costs for a computer are only the beginning. They do not begin to account for all the initial costs involved in purchasing a church computer system.

The Bottom Line

The significant question for your church becomes: "What is the bottom line?" It is difficult to make a generalized statement about what the bottom-line initial costs for your church computer are going to be. The cost of computer hardware and software fluctuates widely depending upon competition and new technological developments. Marketplace trends have shown that hardware costs are generally decreasing, but software costs are generally increasing. So, that trend brings us back to the basic bottom-line issue.

The bottom-line cost for your church depends entirely upon the computer configuration selected. To arrive at the bottom-line cost, the study committee will need to add together the costs of three areas: software, hardware, and miscellaneous items. Using this result, the study committee can then subjectively decide if the benefits of improved church ministry justify the dollar expenditure.

Ideally, a church computer operation should require little technical expertise among the church's staff. In order to achieve this, certain software and hardware minimums are necessary. The following listing contains the basic computer components essential to an effective church computer operation without needing an expert on the church staff. (This listing could be expanded if the church's information requirements demonstrated such a need.)

1. **Software.**
    a. Operating system (CP/M, CP/M-86, MS-DOS, Unix).
    b. Church software.
    c. Word processing, if not included in church software.
2. **Hardware.**
    a. CPU and keyboard. The CPU should have at least 64K core memory, with 128K preferred.
    b. Television monitor.
    c. Two floppy disk drives.
    d. Printer—dot matrix or letter quality depending upon the church needs.
3. **Optional.**
    a. Communications software.
    b. Modem at 300 and/or 1200 baud.
    c. Special needs such as 80-column display circuit board.

After the appropriate software has been selected and the

committee knows its cost, the hardware will fall into place. From these two items, a determination of the initial software and hardware costs can be made by adding the two together.

However, the initial costs also include other items that are related to the computer itself and are needed for an efficient installation and start-up. These include:

1. **Materials.**
   a. Initial supply of computer paper.
   b. Mailing labels.
   c. Floppy disks, minimum of ten disks in the beginning.
   d. Printer ribbons.
   e. Miscellaneous items such as floppy disks files, self-adhesive labels for disks, etc.

2. **Environment.** (See chapter 10 for a detailed discussion of this subject.)
   a. New electrical lines.
   b. Air conditioning and humidity controls.
   c. Building a computer room.

3. **Communications.**
   a. New telephone line installation for the computer. This will allow the church to access large data bases and send electronic mail. A separate telephone line may be necessary if you don't want the church's regular telephone line tied up with the computer.
   b. Modem. (See appendix 1 for a detailed discussion about modems.)

Each of these is relatively inexpensive compared to the initial software and hardware costs. However, they are part of the total installation costs that should be included in the church's planning. After the committee has determined the costs of software, hardware, and related computer start-up items, the bottom-line initial cost can be calculated.

Long-Term Costs

The second type of cost for a computer operation involves long-term expenditures. It is a myth that once the initial costs have been paid out there will be no more expenses for the computer. When an automobile is purchased, gas and oil, lubrication, upkeep, and insurance are necessary items for the efficient operation of the car. In the same way long-term expenditures are necessary for the efficient operation of a computer system. A computer requires "care and feeding," and care and feeding cost money.

Experience in both religious and secular organizations has demonstrated that computers do not necessarily save money in every situation over the long term. In fact, it has been shown that total budgets tend to be slightly higher than they were without computers. Thus, the question becomes: What is the money we thought we would save used for? This question assumes that money is saved by a computer. In fact, some money is saved in certain areas by using a computer. However, this savings is usually redistributed within the organization to one single area: the computer operation. In other words, the money you believed would be saved is consumed by the long-term costs of the computer operation and may slightly increase the bottom-line budget of the church.

Within the church, long-term computer costs can be split into two categories. The first of these includes the costs your church will *definitely* have for a computer operation. These are:

1. **Software support.**
   a. Purchase of new software, whether obtained through a vendor or programmed specifically for your church.
   b. Training in the use of new software.
   c. Modifications to existing software as the information needs of the church change.
   d. Correction of errors or "bugs" in existing software.
2. **Materials.** The church will need a continuous supply of the items listed in the start-up materials area of the initial cost section. This includes paper, labels, floppy disks, ribbons, etc.

Concerning the floppy disks, the committee should plan for at least twice as many disks as you need. For example, if the church is using twenty disks for software and data, a supply of at least forty disks is necessary. These extra disks are used for back-ups, and to replace old floppies that eventually wear out. (See chapter 9.)

3. **Hardware maintenance.** As described in chapter 7, the church should plan for one of the following types:
   a. On-site either through a service contract or on a "time and materials" basis. Service contracts usually cost between 1 percent and 2 percent *per month* of the original *hardware* price.
   b. Depot, i.e., where the computer is physically taken or shipped to a repair facility. The charges for this would be on a "time and materials" basis plus shipping costs to and from the repair facility.

4. **Environment.** This long-term cost is primarily related to the electrical consumption of the computer. In most microcomputers this is minimal. Another cost in this area may be for air conditioning and/or humidity controls required for the computer.

The second category of long-term cost involves expenditures the church may have to support the computer operation. This cost will depend upon the size of your church and its computerization needs. Included in this category are:

1. **Staff,** i.e., programmer and/or operator should your computer operation warrant it.

2. **Communications.**
   a. Monthly rental for the telephone line.
   b. Service contract on the modem if you purchased it, or rental fees if the church leases it from the local telephone company.
   c. Connect charges to the commercially available data bases and electronic mail systems. This is usually a per-hour cost depending upon the service you are using.

    d. Long distance toll calls if you are calling a computer that is not in your local telephone exchange.

As you are probably beginning to grasp, the cost of a computer operation is significant. The reality of dollar expenditures for an effective church computer operation may have a momentous impact upon the total church budget. Therefore, thoughtful analysis and planning are required.

It is natural to wonder at this point what the real value of a church computer truly is. If a computer doesn't save money for an organization and costs so much to operate, what is its major benefit? Computers save massive amounts of time, thereby increasing efficiency and effectiveness. For the church, this means the computer can care for mundane "administrivia," freeing its workers to respond more quickly and effectively to human needs. At the same time, the computer can provide more useful information to church workers in order to improve that response.

A Long-Term Budgeting Guideline

At this point you may feel a bit discouraged and wonder how to plan adequately for these costs. How can the study committee possibly estimate the long-term costs when they have never had a computer? Isn't this a case of which comes first—the chicken or the egg?

In many ways, this is a chicken/egg dilemma. However, your church can benefit from the experience of others. To help your church and study committee with this difficult problem, a general guideline from other computer operations may be useful. The church should expect to spend approximately three times the original purchase price of the computer over a five year period for sustaining the computer operation. This figure includes the original cost of the machine.

For example, the following illustration may help to clarify this general guideline. If your church purchased a computer for $5,000, it should be expected that the computer will cost

$15,000 over a five year period. This means that $10,000 in long-term costs will be required for the church's computer operation during the next five years. In other words, the church budget must account for $167 per month for the computer.

This three-times-over-five-years' guideline is simply that—a guideline. It is not meant to be a long-term computer budgeting rule that applies to all church situations. After your church has actually had the computer in operation for a year or two, the exact long-term costs will become more clear. It will then be possible for your church to properly budget for the computer in its overall planning processes. The guideline given above hopefully will help the church in planning for the long-term costs during at least the first year or two of the church's computer operation.

Financing Alternatives

Beyond the initial and long-term costs of the computer, there is the practical question of how to finance the operation. The long-term costs should be included in your regular budget. However, several options are available for a church to initially finance a computer system. These are:

1. If one, two, or three church members have a great interest in a computer for the church, then it may be feasible for them to purchase the entire computer and donate it to the church. This naturally depends upon the financial resources of the persons involved. The committee may also wish to consider how this alternative could present political or ownership problems in the future.
2. It may be possible for someone in the congregation to purchase the computer and then lease it back to the church. If this option seems feasible, careful thought should be given about long-term costs and other issues. For example, if the hardware breaks down, who is responsible? What happens if the person leasing the

computer leaves the community? Can the church then purchase the computer or continue the lease?

3. A fund drive could raise the money needed for the initial computer costs.

4. If your church has an endowment fund or significant reserves, the computer could be purchased from those funds.

5. It may be possible to arrange for a lease/purchase agreement or straight lease from the vendor. However, questions similar to those in number 2 above would need to be clarified.

In a lease/purchase agreement, you contract with the vendor to pay a monthly fee for thirty-six to sixty months. Then, at the end of the agreed upon period, the church would either own the computer or have the option of purchasing it for a specified "balloon" payment. The monthly fee usually includes some interest so that at the end of the period, the church will have paid between two and three times the original cost of the computer.

6. If someone in the congregation already owns a personal computer, he or she may agree to sell computer time to the church.

7. You may be able to arrange for the vendor to make an outright donation of hardware and software to the church.

Other financing alternatives suited to your own local church situation may be available. These options plus the ones listed above will need analysis so that the best financing choice is made.

No matter how your church computer operation is financed, its cost will probably exceed what you originally had anticipated. In other words, when discussing the cost of a computer operation, expect the unexpected. Careful analysis and planning are essential so that most of the dollar costs for your church's computer can be determined.

Chapter 9
MANAGEMENT
OR MISMANAGEMENT?

Every computer operation requires a certain level of practicality to produce management information valuable to the organization. Whether located in a religious or secular environment, large and small computer installations alike must be administered in ways that generate the greatest benefit to those using the machine. These management details or questions are especially important for a church in order to insure the orderly development of an effective church management information system.

A Ten-Year Miracle

As the study committee wrestles with the management/administrative questions, cognizance of one caution will help: don't expect a miracle overnight. In other words, don't expect the computer to do all the work by itself, *even if* your computer operation is properly administered. Frequently it has been implied that a computer is going to solve all of the church's administrative problems. This simply is not true. In reality, a computer may add to them. At the very least, for the first several years of a computer operation, unique administrative problems are presented not previously experienced in most churches.

A church computer operation evolves, grows, and changes over a period of years. If your church attempted to implement every application on the list in chapter 5, a period of approximately five to seven years would be needed. This time frame includes full software development (or purchase), training, testing, and complete data entry. In fact, one to two years will be required just to fully understand the general ledger, pledge accounting, and membership data systems.

In light of this, the church's study committee may wish to use the phrase "don't expect a miracle overnight" as its theme! Expect a miracle to occur in five to ten years. Expect a useful management information system to become reality several years after the computer is installed. However, as your computer is installed, expect to call upon one of God's most precious gifts: patience. It takes a great amount of time and enduring adjustment to make a computer work for the church.

Management Questions

Due to the lengthy adjustment period, the management of a church computer operation should be efficient and effective. Rules and procedures surrounding your computer operation should be written out and easily accessible to everyone concerned. They should be clearly understood and state precisely "who, what, when, where, and how" about the computer's use.

In planning for a church computer, you should contemplate several issues before acting upon them. Some of the questions discussed in this section may not be applicable to your situation. However, each should be thoughtfully analyzed to determine its potential benefit to your church.

1. **Daily computer operations.**
   a. Who provides for and supervises the day-to-day operation of the computer within the church? (See number 5.)
   b. How is the daily operation executed? For example, who turns the computer on in the morning?
   c. Who is responsible for turning it off at the end of the day?

    d. Who "runs" the back-up procedures? (See number 6.)

    e. Who answers simple questions such as, "What do I do next with this program?"

2. **Church computer operators.**

    a. Who will be the designated operators of the computer? The pastor, secretary, or a volunteer?

    b. If the church secretary is expected to learn how to use the computer and has not used a computer previously, will the church pay for the training?

    c. Often, computer operation is a new skill for the support staff of a church.

       1. Will the church provide salary increases commensurate with the new computer skills learned?

       2. Will job descriptions be upgraded to reflect the new skills?

    d. Who are the back-up operators during vacations and illnesses?

3. **Computer supplies.**

    a. Who makes the decision about ordering supplies?

    b. How often should supplies be ordered?

    c. What is an acceptable safety margin in your supplies inventory when they get low?

    d. What procedures are used for ordering supplies?

    e. Will ordering computer supplies be handled in a similar manner as other church supplies, or will it be controlled differently?

    f. What companies will the supplies be ordered from? Most church suppliers do not carry the extensive array of computer supplies your church will need.

4. **Priorities of software development.**

    • Many well-meaning church members who want to use the computer will believe their need is the most important. These needs are all probably excellent and would produce great benefits for the church. However, if the church has ten persons with three computer ideas each, individually those persons may not fully understand what others want. Thus, ten people with three ideas each means thirty new applications to be developed and implemented! This is a rather strange geometric progression, to say the least. Therefore, controls must be created and software development priorities established because all the ideas, as fine as they may be, obviously can't all be done at once.

- Some questions to consider:
  a. Who decides what the priorities of software development will be?
  b. Who gets what and when do they get it?
  c. Who will decide what need is the most important on the list of remaining applications?
  d. How will such a decision be made? What factors will be taken into account?

5. **Management by committee or individual.**

- Should the computer operation management be done by a small committee or by one person? This may be a possible role for the pastor to assume because he or she is generally defined as the chief administrative officer of the church. While some pastors may be willing to accept this role, there will be others who will not. Some may legitimately claim that they didn't attend seminary and enter the ministry to be a computer manager.
- This decision should be kept fluid and understood by all concerned. The competency of the person responsible for overall computer management and daily operations will either make or break the church's automated MIS. In addition, this policy should be carefully and clearly stated to a new pastor who may wish to suggest changes.

6. **Back-ups.**

- How frequently should a *back-up* be executed? A back-up produces a copy of all information maintained by the computer on an additional disk or tape so that if a disaster occurs while the computer is operating, the current church information will not be lost.

- A disaster is anything that might destroy the computer or its information beyond repair. These could include:
  a. A fire.
  b. An explosion.
  c. Water leakage.
  d. A lightning strike.
  e. Human error.
- In the case of human error, the computer is not physically damaged. Rather, an operator not knowing what to do enters an "erase" command causing some or all of the church's data to disappear. In other words, the computer doesn't have any valid information making it necessary to use the back-up data to continue operations.
- It is a good procedure to "run" or execute a back-up on a daily basis, usually in the late afternoon. You could also choose to run a back-up each week or month, or not at all.
- The key question concerning back-ups is risk. How much or how far are you willing to risk the loss of your church's information? How important is that information to the church? If it is highly important, then you should execute a back-up every day. On the other hand, if you decide that the information in the computer doesn't really mean anything for the ministry of the church or have any bearing on your church work, then don't ever do a back-up. Of course, the logical question in this case is: Why would you have a church computer in the first place if the information didn't mean anything? Back-ups are essential for the operation of a computer in any church.
- As the church begins its computer operation, a back-up once or twice each week may be sufficient. However, as the operation evolves and grows, the back-up fre-

quency should be increased. Eventually the church should complete a daily back-up to protect its information.

- The church should also provide for off-site back-up storage. Each week, usually on Fridays, a second back-up should be completed. This back-up copy is then stored off site in a safety deposit box or other secure location. This protective control will give the church a copy of all current information if a totally destructive disaster occurs; for example, the church burns to the ground. Should the unthinkable happen, you can use the off-site back-up copy, access another computer of similar design in another location, and continue your operations.

- As the church plans for its back-up procedures, it will need at least twice as many floppy disks as are needed for actual data. In other words, one floppy holds data and one floppy serves as a back-up. Therefore, if the church has ten floppy disks with software and church information, a total of twenty disks is needed—ten masters and ten back-ups.

- If the church has a hard disk with floppy disk back-up, then the size of the hard disk must be divided by the floppy disk size to determine the number of floppies needed. For example, if the church has a 10MB hard disk with a 500K floppy disk drive, then at least twenty floppy disks are required for back-up. The same formula is true if the church has a hard disk with tape back-up.

- As a general rule of thumb, it is always a good idea to have five or ten extra floppy disks or one or two additional tapes available. These can be used in emergencies, or as extra back-ups.

7. **Disaster recovery plan.**
   - Disaster recovery is an issue related to back-ups. In case of a disaster, what plan can be used to provide for

an efficient recovery of your computer operation? It is advisable to find some other person or business locally with a similar computer and write a disaster recovery agreement with them, **before** the unhappy event of a disaster. This agreement would make the other computer available for the church's processing if a disaster occurred.

- The agreement should include:
    a. What constitutes a disaster, e.g., flood, lightning strike, etc.
    b. Priorities of who uses the computer.
    c. When it can be used.
    d. How many hours each day it will be available.
    e. Who is permitted access to the computer.
    f. When it should be reasonably expected that a new computer can be secured for the "injured party."
    g. A reciprocity clause so that either side may be able to use the other's computer in a disaster.
    h. Other practical details relevant to such an agreement and plan.

8. **Security.**
    - Who has access to the information in the computer? Or more precisely, who has access to what information in the computer? Some churches may find it necessary to allow only certain designated persons access to the computer. Others may say that everyone in the church can have access, but that passwords and identification numbers will be used to protect various pieces of information.
    - Naturally you may wonder why computer security is important for the church. What information does the church want to hide? This is not the issue, because no church organization should ever have anything to hide or cover up. Rather, computer security in a church environment protects the church's information from damage or loss. The purpose of computer security in the church is to protect the integrity and accuracy of

the church's information. It is easy to imagine a person without the proper knowledge becoming trapped in a program and simply turning the computer's power off to get out of the problem. However, if the floppy disks are operating at that moment, the information on those disks may be lost because the power was cut and the disks were scratched by the read/write heads as they retracted. (This is also another reason to complete timely back-ups.)

- Using the computer in the church school also adds a special dimension to the security issue. In this situation, many children and adults will have access to the computer. It would be wise to lock up those floppy disks with crucial church information in a filing cabinet. The problem here again is not intentional damage to the church's information, but an unknowledgeable person making an honest mistake that destroys or damages some of the church's information.

- On the other hand, if a person with formidable knowledge about computers holding a grudge against your church gains access to the computer, massive damage to the church's information could occur. While you may see this as a remote possibility, my own experience in computer positions with two secular, nonprofit public institutions saw incidents of personal grudge and revenge occur to the organization's computerized data. Thus, it is wise for a church to establish computer security and other precautions prior to the computer's installation as well as completing regular back-ups.

9. **Church programmer.**

- Every church has specialized information needs that may require customized software. Even though a software package is initially selected to meet the church's needs, you may eventually outgrow it as needs change. Also, software available from your local computer store may not meet the changing computer needs of the church. Thus, a church computer programmer may ultimately be required to fulfill the increasing information demands of the church. A church programmer can be found through volunteers, students, or in the professional computer ranks.

- It is true that local churches rely very heavily on volunteers, and this may be a viable option for computer programming in your church. Someone in the congregation with programming skills could possibily provide software development and support for new systems that the church needs. This can be an inexpensive method of gaining efficient software for the church.

- However, the management team or computer manager must make a decision about who will be the church's volunteer programmer. For example, what happens if your volunteer programmer dies or moves out of the community? If there is no back-up programmer, the church may have perhaps one or two years' worth of software development not yet complete, and therefore essentially worthless to the church.

- A true story may help illustrate this problem. There is a large church that installed a $30,000 computer. The computer was purchased primarily due to the promise of a well-meaning church member—he would provide software development and support. This person was very genuine and honest in making such an offer. On the other hand, the study committee did not allow for the fact that this person was also extremely competent and in a great deal of demand.

- After the computer had been installed for three months and was not yet functioning, their volunteer programmer was offered another job, accepted it, and moved across the country. There they were, high and dry with a $30,000 computer, three months of software development, maintenance costs, materials, and numerous other computer-related items all essentially worthless. They had not developed a contingency plan for this problem and were at a loss in deciding what to do next.

- After reading this, you may be discouraged about using *any* volunteers for your computer operation. Please don't be. Well-intentioned and committed volunteers *can* be used for your church's computer, if the proper controls are established. The study committee will need to carefully analyze and plan such controls that the best possible use of computer volunteers and students can be achieved.

- Another alternative for church programming is through a trade school or college. Many churches are located by or near a college or university with computer science programs, or in areas that have programmer trade schools. Frequently students from these institutions are available to computer installations through work/study opportunities. Your church could take advantage of such a plan if your church is located within twenty-five miles of a college or trade school campus. This is a way to obtain inexpensive software for the church that will assist the church to meet its growing needs.

- However, there are disadvantages to this plan. Students are just that—students. They are learning, and your church computer operation is the laboratory. The church may obtain a great deal of software through this method, but some of its quality may be questionable. This is not because students aren't competent; rather they are learning through their mistakes. Also, because students are so mobile, once they have left the area, long-term support of the software will probably become nonexistent.

- If the study committee feels that computer volunteers or students should not be used in your situation, then the church will have to:
  a. employ a programmer on the staff, or

b. contract with a free-lance programmer in your community, or

c. retain a local software house with programming expertise.

Each of these alternatives will be much more expensive than using volunteers or students. However, the committee may feel that the benefits of long-term support and better quality are worth the extra dollar expenditures.

10. **Documentation.**

- Documentation is another management concern to consider. Documentation is written material and manuals that explain about the computer hardware and software. It will show how to turn the computer's power on and off, how the programs work, and give the operator instructions. All documentation should be provided by the software programmer or the hardware/software vendor. If volunteer or student programmers are used, the church must insist upon documentation being provided as one of the controls. If the church contracts the work to a free-lance programmer or software house, the contract should include a clause about payment being withheld until documentation is provided.

- Documentation is an absolute requirement for understanding the operation of any computer system. It is also highly important and immensely helpful when change occurs among the staff (i.e., the pastor, the secretary, church school teachers, and the programmer.) As new staff are employed, documentation allows the new person to become familiar with the computer and its operation more quickly, requiring less training time. Documentation is essential for the continued and efficient operation of the computer system in the church.

11. **Computer user's group.**

- It may be advisable to form a church computer user's

group within the congregation. This group could be called the "Computer Advisory Committee" (CAC) or any other appropriate name. A CAC can listen to the needs of the congregation and suggest ways that the computer can be used in meeting those needs. This data can be provided to the management team concerning what applications should be developed and when they should be implemented on the computer.

- A users' group or CAC will also assist the congregation to sort out their priorities. For example, is it more important in your church to start a general ledger/pledge accounting system than it is to have the computer used in the church school? The treasurer and financial secretary might feel finances are more important. The church school teachers and superintendent might feel that the church school is more important. Having a CAC will allow these persons to negotiate various priorities, suggesting to the management team who gets what and when they get it. Also, a CAC provides a forum in that various church officers may come to understand what another person does in support of the church's overall ministry. It has been observed that the commonality of computer use forces the human beings in an organization to communicate much better. A CAC may produce for your church the unexpected benefit of increasing teamwork through a common ministry and discipleship. Wouldn't it be ironic if modern technology forces the church to do what Jesus asked us to do in the first place?

12. **Computer training.**
    - Training in the computer's use has been previously discussed; however, it is presented here again as it relates to overall management of the computer operation. Some questions to consider:
        a. Who in the church will be trained to use the computer?

    b. How much training is required?

    c. Who provides the training, and where is it held?

    d. What does the training cost?

13. **Initial data entry.**

    • What plans will be made for initial data entry? Initial data entry is a very time-consuming process after computer installation. Information about all the members must be entered. This would include names, addresses, birthdays, baptisms, pledges, etc., etc. The list really seems endless, and doesn't include general ledger financial data, property inventory, etc. Yet, in order for your computer to become a valuable tool, the data obviously must be entered. Thus, plans must be made to accomplish this laborious, and perhaps herculean, task. Some questions to consider:

    a. Who will complete the data entry?

    b. Will the regular church secretary complete this task? If so, how will the normal secretarial duties be continued?

    c. Will the pastor complete the data entry, or is this a poor use of his or her time?

    d. Will the church use volunteers for this task?

    e. Will the church employ temporary support staff to accomplish this?

    f. After the data is entered, will someone verify its accuracy? How often should such a verification be done? Every day, week, or month?

The management issues discussed above are serious considerations for your church. They have far-reaching implications that need prayerful analysis and planning. The dollar cost of these management issues will be relatively minimal, but your cost in time to implement them will be great. Regardless of your congregation's size, your answers to these questions are essential to the efficient, effective, and propitious use of a computer in your church.

Chapter 10

AN UNRELATED
BUT DYNAMIC DUO

There are two important considerations for a church computer operation that are frequently overlooked since they are often thought of as "sideshows" to the real computer operation. However, to adequately plan for your church computer, you must deliberate upon them so that your church's computer installation will be successful.

Physical Environment

The first of these considerations is the computer's physical environment. It may be hard to imagine, but many computers require special rooms with air conditioning, raised floors, sensitive humidity controls, and static-free air. Such exotic physical requirements are usually limited to large mainframe and minicomputers. However, it is also true that many microcomputers suitable for a church have certain physical requirements, the very least of which is a sturdy table large enough to hold it. Environment can be crucial to the church's computer installation because the hardware selected may require certain temperature, humidity, and electrical parameters even if your machine is a microcomputer.

There are three questions about environment that the church should ask of its hardware vendor:

1. **In what temperature range does the computer function?**
   - Many computers cannot operate efficiently if the temperature exceeds 80 or 85 degrees. If you live in a

climate where summer temperatures go above this limit, and the room that houses your computer does not have air conditioning, the computer can be damaged.

2. **What is the range of humidity in which the computer is operational?**

   • Some computers cannot function well in high humidity situations, especially above 80 percent. If you live in a humid area and you don't have humidity control (air conditioning), the computer may be harmed.

   • In addition, if the computer is located in a basement room that tends to be damp, the computer could be injured if operated. Investment in a dehumidifier is advisable in this situation.

3. **What electrical requirements are necessary for the computer?**

   • Some vendors require that *each* of their computers and *peripheral* devices (i.e., disk drives, monitor, etc.) have "dedicated" electrical lines. These are lines free of any other electrical devices such as typewriters, copy machines, electric pencil sharpeners, florescent lights, etc. If this is true, you need to employ an electrician to install dedicated electrical lines. Other vendors indicate that any normal 110 or 120 volt, 15 to 30 hertz line is sufficient, and that other electrical devices on the same line as the computer will not cause any problems.

The bottom line about physical environment can be reduced to a question: What remodeling will be necessary in your building to install the computer, and what will it cost? Obviously, this is an initial cost that must be accounted for in the entire computer purchase. If it is necessary to install dedicated electrical lines, a special air conditioning unit, temperature controls, or a dehumidifier, you will have to spend some money. This needs to be planned for as the committee develops cost estimates and a budget for the computer.

Also related to the question of remodeling is where the

computer will actually be located in the church building. The study committee will need to examine available areas in the building and decide what location would be most advantageous to all church operations. It may be necessary to build a separate computer room; however, such a decision can be made only after the proper analysis.

If the study committee decides to locate the computer system in the secretary's office, special care should be used. Some computer printers generate sufficient noise to interrupt concentration or drown out a person on the telephone. This could be a difficulty for the secretary and others who use the office on a regular basis. Thus, the committee may wish to ask the secretary and others how they would feel about the noise. If possible, a demonstration of the printer in the secretary's office would help him or her determine if the noise level is tolerable.

While many microcomputers today are considered desk-top size, most require a space larger than a desk. It is generally a good idea to have a small room for your computer operation separate from your other operations. At the very least, a large table anywhere from seven to nine feet in length is advisable. This table should be able to accommodate the computer itself, printer, monitor, disk drives, other components, necessary supplies, manuals and documentation for operating the system, and work space to lay papers, etc. Also, if you will be using the computer in telecommunications, space near the computer for a telephone and modem will be required.

The aspect of environment for the computer may not have even entered your previous thoughts about church computers. In fact, this may seem ancillary to your main concerns; however, the computer's location can play a major part in its success or failure. If the location chosen is the secretary's or pastor's office, possessiveness or ownership of the machine can be detrimental to its intended use. Thus, the overriding concern in location is to determine where the computer best fulfills your church's needs.

Obsolescence

The other major area that strikes fear in the hearts of computer consumers is obsolescence. A great deal is said today about obsolete computer hardware. Many persons naturally wonder if a certain computer being considered for purchase would be obsolete even before it is delivered. This is a legitimate concern that the church must deal with if it is going to employ computers. America's notorious "throw-away" society has not allowed the computer world to escape the clutches of built-in obsolescence.

There are two types of obsolescence for churches to think about:

1. **Technological obsolescence.** It should be expected that any computer installed today will be obsolete in the marketplace within four or five years due to new technological advancements. As a result, after your church's computer has been installed, it is quite likely that your vendor and even some well-meaning church members will be giving you friendly, but perhaps unwanted advice: you have an obsolete computer.

2. **Functional obsolescence.** Functional obsolescence depends upon how quickly you outgrow the capabilities of the computer you have installed. Functional obsolescence is directly related to the church's internal computer operation. Generally, this is not dependent upon technological obsolescence.

As an example, one of the judicatory bodies in a mainline denomination purchased a computer in 1968. In 1983, they were still using this computer in spite of the fact that it was a technologically obsolete machine. However, during the fifteen years the computer was in their office, it continued to meet their needs. They were able to program new applications on the computer to fulfill their growing needs.

After fifteen years, however, they reluctantly installed a new computer. The only reason this office purchased a new machine was because the manufacturer informed them service on their computer would no longer be available after January 1, 1984. Thus, they were forced into technological obsolescence even though their computer was not functionally obsolete.

As long as the computer in your church meets your needs and can be serviced, *it is not obsolete* no matter what anyone may say. A vendor, programmer, or church member may be saying that your church's computer is obsolete, and something ought to be done about it. But, it may not, in fact, be obsolete. Your computer may meet the church's needs for fifteen or twenty years regardless of what is happening in the computer marketplace. Therefore, obsolescence should be weighed in a balance between technological and functional. Care should be taken not to place the church into the cost-wasting position of replacing a perfectly good computer before it really needs to.

Chapter 11

THE BIG PICTURE

As you contemplate the overall requirements of a computer for your church, it may help to read a summary of what has been discussed previously. With all the details necessary in planning for, selecting, installing, and implementing a church computer, you may feel as if you can't see the forest for the trees. Thus, this section attempts to provide a more complete view of what you are considering—the big picture.

These next few paragraphs offer:

1. A list of briefly summarized, but important factors used in purchasing a total computer system.
2. A generalized plan for church automation.

You will recognize most of the points in each of these because they have been presented in various ways throughout previous chapters.

Factors

Table 11-1 contains a list of factors important to any decision about a church computer. This list should provide an overview for the committee studying a church computer purchase.

TABLE 11-1

SOME FACTORS TO CONSIDER IN THE PURCHASE OF A COMPUTER SYSTEM

1. **Versatility.** Are the software and hardware easy to use? Is the computer user friendly?

2. **Reliability.** Do the software and hardware have a good record among other users?

3. **Vendor stability.** Are the vendors you are considering financially stable? Ask to see their financial statements and have them reviewed by your banker. Do they genuinely seem to have the church's interests at heart? Will they stick with you if you run into trouble?

4. **Operating systems and computer languages.** What operating systems and computer languages do the vendors offer with their computers? Are they common or standard so you can take advantage of future developments? Are they so exotic that the church's potential use of the computer will be limited?

5. **Storage capacity.** Will the computer have adequate core and mass storage to meet the church's needs?

6. **Expansion potential.** Is the computer upward compatible so that new hardware and/or software may be added in the future? Will you have to purchase an entirely new computer if the church wants to add a hard disk or additional terminal?

7. **Standardization.** Are the hardware and software standardized to denominational suggestions or requirements?

8. **Hardware maintenance.** Is service for the hardware through an on-site or depot method?

9. **Software support.** What long-term software support is available, and what does it cost?

10. **Cost.** What is the total initial cost? What are the estimated long-term costs? How will the costs be financed?

11. **Physical environment.** Are any special temperature, humidity, and electrical requirements necessary for the computer? If so, what are they, and what needs to be done in the church building to meet them?

12. **Training.** What hardware and software training is available from the vendor? Is any training included

with the purchase? How much? What will future training cost? Where is it held?

Plan for Church Automation

A general plan for church automation is shown in Table 11-2. Other very good plans for computerizing a church's information system also exist, and the outline presented here is by no means *the* way to automate your church. Rather, this outline reflects my understanding and opinions of the steps required in computerizing that part of Christendom which is your church. This plan can be adapted to fit any particular church situation with pieces added or deleted as necessary. In any case, it is designed to give you a beginning to end (or is it beginning to beginning) view of placing a computer in your church.

Also, one further note—this plan is presented in staggered chronological order. In other words, some points will occur simultaneously in your study process, and in some instances certain tasks begin as others conclude.

TABLE 11-2

GENERAL PLAN FOR CHURCH AUTOMATION

I. Begin study process
    A. Educate decision makers
    B. Perform needs analysis
    C. Develop rationale for a computer in your church
    D. State benefits
       1. Practical
       2. Ministry
    E. Cost analysis for better stewardship
       1. Savings in time
       2. Savings in dollars
II. Prepare specifications
    A. Define general configuration to meet needs stated in I. B.

  1. Software
  2. Hardware
  B. Estimate initial costs
  C. Choose method of financing
  D. Prepare a general plan of computer operation management
III. Software
  A. Evaluate based on needs stated in I. B.
  B. Select
IV. Hardware
  A. Evaluate based on software selected in III. B.
  B. Select
V. Cost and location control
  A. Choose location
  B. Estimate remodeling costs
  C. Finalize initial cost estimate
  D. Estimate long-term costs
VI. Final recommendations and approvals
  A. Make recommendations to proper administrative church bodies
  B. Gain all required approvals
VII. Prepare for installation
  A. Order system and specify delivery date
  B. Complete required remodeling
  C. Design and implement a specific management plan
  D. Create user's group
VIII. Integrate computer system into the church
  A. Install and check out computer
  B. Train operators in software and hardware use
  C. Data entry
  D. Care for all adjustment details
IX. Begin management information system
  A. Use computer to produce beneficial information
  B. Continue management plan implementation
  C. Meet with users periodically and adjust priorities

Chapter 12

COMPUTERS IN
THE CHURCH SCHOOL?

The Sunday school or church school has long been a tradition and method of evangelism for the vast majority of churches. However, it is also one of the most difficult areas in the church to prepare for because of heavy reliance upon volunteers. Coupled with this is a lack of training or interest on the part of many pastors placing the church school in a lesser priority than many other tasks. Yet, most churches at one time or another will place an emphasis upon the church school and its development. When this happens, computer technology could become a very important tool that might enliven dull classes, produce new interest, and generate a flurry of creativity in both teachers and students. Indeed, one of the greatest potential uses of a computer in a local church is in the church school. In the future, *Computer Based Education* (CBE) could become the most significant use of a computer in the church.

Computer Based Education is a concept that has existed since the early 1960s. Significant research has been done by universities and other educational institutions on how computers can assist the learning process in the schools. The impressive findings indicate that CBE results in learning of at least the same level as by conventional teaching methods. However, no major studies have been done of CBE in the church school environment because adequate CBE facilities do not exist in church schools.

Because the church school environment is similar to any public or private classroom environment, the teaching techniques used in the church school can be the same as in a regular classroom while the content and the student population are different. Thus, CBE can easily be adapted to the church school.

According to Richard C. Atkinson and H. A. Wilson in their book *Computer Assisted Instruction: A Book of Readings,* the primary aim of Computer Based Education is "to optimize the learning process." In other words, the computer is used to enhance and possibly improve the ways in which any adult or child learns.

Branches of CBE

There are two major branches or types of Computer Based Education:

1. **Computer Assisted Instruction (CAI).** CAI primarily relates to the actual learning process between computer and student. The computer is used directly by the student in ways to facilitate learning.
2. **Computer Managed Instruction (CMI).** CMI is used by the teacher to care for the administrative and organizational details of the class. The computer is used indirectly in the learning process as an aid primarily for the teacher's benefit.

Computer Assisted Instruction

Computer Assisted Instruction is a concept whereby students use the computer in an individual manner to either learn a new concept or reinforce one previously learned in the classroom situation. Often CAI approximates or simulates teacher-student interaction as a concept is presented and learned.

CAI Modes

There are four modes or types of CAI. These are:
1. **Problem solving.**
   - In the problem solving mode of CAI, a student utilizes the computer to find solutions to problems using

general principles and concepts learned previously in the classroom. Problem solving CAI makes the assumption that the student has expertise with some computer programming language and therefore writes a computer program for solving the problem.

- This mode has its greatest potential in the sciences, engineering, and mathematics where problems often involve long and complex mathematical manipulations. Because the computer can do rapid computations, the student is able to examine more complicated and realistic problems than would be possible with a manual system. It is claimed that a student gains a deeper understanding of the problem and of the concept involved as a result of analyzing more complicated problems. An example of problem solving in the church school environment would be in teaching good stewardship through proper budgeting. However, the student must know how to program the computer or have in-depth knowledge of common "spreadsheet" programs.

2. **Simulation.**
   - The simulation mode of CAI is used to provide a model of a real situation on the computer where the student is placed in a decision-making role. The main purpose of any simulation is to duplicate events that occur in the real world while at the same time following an instructional process that causes the student to learn. Simulations can also be used extensively in health training programs such as medicine and dentistry, and in aerospace training for pilots and astronauts. Other examples of simulation might include:
     a. Playing out the scenario of a nuclear holocaust where the student must make the decision whether or not to push the button that sends the missiles.
     b. A model of the national economy designed to examine the effects of certain government policies

where the student is president of a bank, or perhaps the owner of a small business.

c. A model of the nation's voters, which assists in the evaluation and development of political campaign strategies where the student is the candidate.

• Computer simulations in the church school might be used to raise the social and moral awareness about the pros and cons of nuclear war, the economy, unemployment, and other important issues today. A group of church school students could individually use a certain simulation, each making different decisions based upon their life perspectives as the computer presents situations and scenarios. Then, they could gather as a class to discuss their simulation experiences and what they learned as a result. Each student will see the consequences of their decisions and how they affect others. From this, a sense of community is developed through the willingness to exchange ideas and understand the moral implications of individual actions.

3. **Drill and practice.**

• In the drill and practice mode of CAI, the computer supplements teacher instruction by drilling students on previously learned facts and concepts. This helps the student in practicing and developing proficiency in certain skills. The drill and practice mode is very much like the old flash card method frequently used in elementary schools.

• Through the drill and practice mode, the computer presents a linear sequence of exercises. When these exercises are completed, the computer evaluates the performance, and based upon preprogrammed score levels, the student is assigned new, more difficult drills or is led to remedial materials. Examples of drill and practice include foreign languages, vocabulary, spelling, punctuation, and arithmetic skills.

- CAI drill and practice techniques could be used in the church school to assist students in remembering Bible facts. This could be a fun way for children and adults to become more familiar with the Bible and the location of important Scripture.

4. **Tutorial.**

- The tutorial mode of CAI is probably that which comes closest to a teacher-student interaction. In the tutorial mode, the computer presents a brand-new concept or concepts, which the student has *never before* experienced. After the concept has been presented, the tutorial can continue by presenting problems and questions designed to synthesize the concept within the student's psyche. This reinforces the new idea and helps a student to develop his or her skills in the concept just learned. The intent of the tutorial mode is to approximate or simulate the actions of a skilled and patient tutor working with an individual student. The tutorial mode also frees the teacher to work with students on an individual basis.

- As mentioned previously, an example of the drill and practice mode is to help a student memorize his or her biblical facts. The tutorial mode, on the other hand, could be used to take those facts and assist in integrating them into a system of learning faith, theology, and moral values for living a Christian life. Also, this CAI mode could easily be applied to the church in numerous situations where the meaning of the church, its history, mission, and ministry needs to be communicated through the church school.

Computer Managed Instruction

The second major area in computer based learning is CMI or Computer Managed Instruction. Computer Managed Instruction assists the teacher with the administrative work required in the teaching process. Through the computer church school, CMI would maintain a data base of information relating to students such as names and addresses, birthdays, whether they have been baptized, attendance records, offerings, etc.

Some examples of CMI in the church school might be:

1. **Student progress reports.** Such a report would assist the church school teacher in tracking individual students and their progress in a particular unit.

2. **Attendance records.** This application could be used to provide the teacher with information regarding absences. A list of students who have missed the class for three or more Sundays could be produced for follow-up purposes. This could be particularly useful in churches where teachers are changed every quarter and the new teacher does not know the records of students in the class.

3. **Offerings.** The computer could maintain a record of offerings for each church school class, provide grand totals, and credit the proper account in the general ledger system used for the entire church. (This is another example of software interfacing discussed in chapter 6.)

4. **Curriculum history.** The computer could maintain a record of what curriculum has been used in what classes during the previous years. Church school teachers sometimes wonder what curriculum their students have been exposed to in previous years. This helps them in lesson planning for the class's current work.

The Advantage of CBE

CBE has one major advantage and three disadvantages significant for the church. Such factors should be taken into account because they may either help or hinder CBE in your church school.

There is one primary advantage of CBE important for the church school teaching process—individualization of the teaching process with students. Educational professionals have felt for quite some time that the ideal teacher-student ratio is one to one. In the public schools, university environment, and church school, this type of individualization is usually not possible because of teacher shortages and the massive funding required for individual instruction. The great majority of students will never experience the benefits of individual instruction unless they enter doctoral level graduate programs or were raised in small one-room schools.

Computers may afford the opportunity of optimizing the learning process (Atkinson and Wilson) by approaching the individualization ideal. This can be of immense benefit for many students especially in deprived and socio-economically depressed areas. It has been demonstrated that students from metropolitan ghetto areas or poor rural areas respond significantly better to computerized instruction than to regular teachers. The basic reason for this is because the computer treats them more like individuals than regular classroom teachers do.

Individualization through CBE allows the student to move through the learning process at his or her own pace. This means the gifted student can travel quickly through material and not be limited by the rest of the students in a class. On the other hand, a slow-learning student can be allowed as much time as is necessary to learn a concept. Self-paced learning considerably reduces the very negative and serious pressure to perform well in a competitive academic sense when each person has differing learning abilities.

A natural criticism of individualization is the negation of the community aspect of Christianity. However, CBE seeks only to individualize the learning process—not the entire socialization of the child or adult. In addition, CBE can be controlled by the church to focus upon learnings that will benefit the entire community. In other words, individualized instruction in the church school can help everyone celebrate their individual God-given gifts and graces. At the same time, everyone can be led into a feeling of community where individual gifts, no matter how small, contribute to the corporate ministry of the entire body of Christ, and where no one is made to feel "bad" because he or she can't keep up with the rest.

The Disadvantages of CBE

There are three disadvantages of Computer Based Education that apply to the church school.

1. **Emotional needs of students.**
   - The computer does not respond to the emotional needs of the students. Computers will never replace a human teacher in the classroom. A computer cannot see a student's face light up when a concept begins to make sense. It cannot see the perplexed look that comes with confusion, or it cannot respond to the student's questioning voice when a difficulty occurs. A computer just plods along not hearing, not seeing, and not knowing what to do with such responses. It just keeps following the preprogrammed instructional software.
   - Over a period of time, if a student has interaction only with computers, serious emotional problems can result. A student cannot become a socially responsible and moral member of society if he or she only interacts with computers. Thus, computers should never replace the church school teacher, but can serve as an instructional tool to create a better learning environment about God and his work.

2. **Time and cost.**
   - Instructional software is very time-consuming and costly to develop. This is true in any educational

situation where CBE is being developed. For example, it has been estimated that a tutorial with one-half hour of student instruction takes between forty and eighty hours of design and programming time.

- Because most churches rely so heavily on untrained teacher volunteers in the church school, this disadvantage will be a major problem. There are two facts that have been documented by Christian educators about volunteer church school teachers:

  a. Most do not prepare their lessons and materials until Saturday evening.

  b. Most spend only one hour or less per week with their lessons.

  Given these facts, it would be practically impossible to get those volunteers to develop appropriate computer instructional software to enhance learning. Most volunteer teachers, in spite of their devotion and dedication, simply do not want to commit the necessary time required for CBE. Thus, the developmental task would be left to denominational boards and agencies *if* the local churches will provide the needed funding to begin and continue such a monumental undertaking.

- In addition, extensive training would be required for church school teachers using the computer for their work. This training would be a costly and lengthy process, once again calling for even more time than most teachers are willing to commit.

- Compounding the training problem is the fact that church school teacher turnover is so high. Because of rapid turnover from one year to the next, computer training would have to be provided each year. This simply escalates the costs for using CBE in the church school. In churches where the teachers change every quarter, training for the new teachers would then have to be provided on a quarterly basis. Again, costs rise, which creates serious questions about the viability of CBE in the church school.

3. **Adequate CBE facilities.**

- An adequate CBE facility is costly and beyond the resources of most churches. If the church purchases one microcomputer for all purposes, the chances are minimal that it could be used at all in the church school. If your church school has only ten students that come for one hour on fifty-two Sundays per year, each student might get to use the computer for thirty minutes every fifth or sixth week. This may be more frustrating than helpful. This is compounded if your church school has, e.g., fifty-two students, which is a more realistic figure for most churches. If every student is given thirty minutes on the computer, then each one would be able to use it only two times per year! This limited access would most certainly counteract the desired CBE benefits.

- An adequate CBE facility really requires many microcomputers or a multi-tasking minicomputer with many terminals. The cost of such an operation would be in the tens of thousands of dollars, again raising serious questions about CBE's feasibility in the church school. (See appendix 1 for a description of multi-task computers.)

In the Final Analysis . . .

In spite of the disadvantages of using CBE in the church school, the church would be ill-advised to ignore its potential benefits. The age of computer literacy is here. Children in the schools are now exposed to computers in kindergarten and first grade, making it even more imperative for the church school to implement CBE. Society will move ahead in spite of what the church does or doesn't do. Thus, if pastors and church boards place priority emphasis upon the church school shifting needed dollars from other areas, CBE could become a reality. Even though one microcomputer may not be adequate, it is a beginning. The church came from a very humble beginning in Bethlehem, and perhaps church school CBE can take its cue from that modest start.

Chapter 13

TECHNOLOGY AND THEOLOGY

Computers in the modern church are viewed in a variety of ways by Christians. These opinions reflect both positive and negative judgments of the continuous twentieth century transformation of technology. Christian perspectives about computers seem to include:

1. The idea that they are mutations of a materialistic society.
2. Computers are a contradiction of the church's mission and therefore not necessary to our ministry.
3. The belief that the installation of a computer in any church is strictly a business decision requiring no discussion of its impact upon Christian theology.
4. The desire in some circles that the church replace its mission with computers making technology the object of faith rather than Jesus Christ.

Is a church computer a mutation, contradiction, business decision, or idol? Obviously, it is not any of these, yet the razzle and dazzle of the computer world may cause Christians to bypass the link between technology and theology. Fascination with the machine may prevent the real essence of computers in the church from being analyzed.

Christians are called constantly to struggle with how faith and theology provide the basis for daily living. Christian discipleship demands that we give *all* of our being to God so that life with Christ becomes a complete reality. Therefore, it seems impossible to separate the use of any church equipment, the church building, the development of any church missional program, or the recruitment of persons to serve on a computer study committee from the theological basis for the church's existence. As the visible body of Christ in the world, the church is called to witness for our Lord in both words and actions using the abundant resources God has provided. Computer technology is one of those twentieth and twenty-first century tools that will make the church's ministry more vital and alive if the linkage between it and theology is probed.

A computer in the church is more than an administrative tool. The church probably should not use computers or, for that matter, copy machines or telephones, unless they serve the work of the church. While a computer is an efficient administrative tool, it is also a resource that should improve the church's ministry. When used properly, computers and other technological devices are designed to save massive amounts of time consumed by church administrivia. Computers can remember minute details of church work, thereby creating a better environment for churches in responding to people. Computers are tools of ministry that allow Christians to make a more rapid and informative response to the human needs of the local congregational and world communities.

Table 13-1 contains a list of questions designed to help your study committee determine how a computer can be integrated into your church's overall ministry. Your church may not be able to find answers to any or all of these questions. That's fine because many theological questions are unanswerable. However, they may help your church to understand, if it hasn't already, how computer technology is a tool for the mission of Jesus Christ.

Discussion of these questions by the study committee may mean the difference between whether the church works for the computer or the computer works for the church. There aren't right or wrong answers to these questions, but your findings will assist the church in understanding a computer's impact. Your committee may discover some disturbing answers. On the other hand, you may find some unexpected ecstasies. In any case, addressing these issues will provide a springboard into the theological and practical relevance of the computer in the church.

TABLE 13-1

SOME FUNDAMENTAL
QUESTIONS ABOUT COMPUTERS IN THE CHURCH

- How would a computer assist in the fulfillment of your church's goals and objectives?
- Can your church justify a computer based on the need to improve ministry through more efficient information control? In other words, does your church *really need* a computer?
- Will a computer simply eliminate manual systems, or will it provide useful information for the ministry of the church?
- Is the dollar and human cost justified by your need for improved information control?
- What is the payback or return on your investment as it relates to the kingdom of God? In other words, what is the major benefit of a computer for your church's ministry?
- Will the computer provide information for a balanced ministry between the personal and social aspects of the gospel?
- How will the computer assist church members to become better stewards of God's gifts and church resources? Will it encourage better discipleship?
- What ethical, moral, and social questions being raised by computer technology will have a direct impact upon your church?

The Human Cost of Computers

In previous chapters, the cost of using a computer was purposely limited to dollars. However, the word *cost* means more than dollars in the church. The study committee may wish to analyze the human cost of computer technology in your church. The basic issue in the human cost question concerns the overall impact of a computer upon the people of your church. There may be little or no negative human consequences, but there could also be a significant effect upon the congregation causing ripples within the church for years.

When examining the human cost questions, the study committee should review what impact a computer may have upon both paid church staff and volunteers. Questions to consider might include:

- How will the staff react to a computer?
- Does any cyberphobia, i.e., fear of the computer, exist among the staff, and how should it be dealt with?
- Does anyone on the staff believe that the computer will take over his or her job? If so, how can this be handled in a compassionate and sensitive way?

Other human cost questions relate to how a computer may be used to control church information that has been maintained manually by volunteers. It is a fact that Christian churches of all denominations rely heavily upon volunteers to do numerous tasks. The committee may wish to analyze what information targeted for automation is maintained by volunteers. From this study, you should be able to determine if the computer will replace any dedicated church volunteers.

A true story may help clarify this issue. Once, there was a church studying how a computer could be used in a variety of tasks. After the needs analysis was completed, the committee determined that the "Ritual of Friendship" forms completed every Sunday by church members and visitors would be put into and maintained in the computer. (The Ritual of Friendship forms are worship attendance records that

identify visitors, newcomers, and the regular church atten-
dees.) This is a perfectly valid application of the computer,
which can assist the staff in tracking the attendance of
members and in easily identifying visitors. Entering the
information from the cards into the computer could save
significant time.

In this church there was a widower and retired business
man who maintained the Ritual of Friendship forms. He
enjoyed this job, and found it to be a way in which he could
offer more to the church than money. For him, it was a real
ministry and a meaningful contribution to the life of the
church.

In listing the Ritual of Friendship as a computer
application, the study committee failed to ask this dedicated
church member if he wanted to give up his volunteer job to a
computer. They just assumed that he would.

Eventually, the final computer proposal was completed and
presented to the church board for approval. The person who
maintained the Ritual of Friendship was also a member of the
board. When he discovered the Ritual of Friendship was listed
as an application for the computer, he exploded. As a former
business man, he believed that the computer was a valid tool
for the work of the church. But he was extremely upset that no
one had talked to him about the computer taking over his
job—a job that he enjoyed and that gave him an outlet of
ministry to the church.

To avoid such an incident from happening in your church,
the committee should use the results of the needs analysis to
determine the impact of a proposed computer. Questions
about a computer's impact upon church volunteers might
include:

- Will the computer replace a volunteer church member's
  job?
- Has the study committee asked those volunteers how
  they feel about the computer's impact upon their
  church work?

• How can the skills and talents of volunteers (or paid staff) be used in other areas of the church if they are displaced by the computer?

In general, how can the computer committee be sensitive and empathetic to the feelings of both volunteers and staff during the transition from manual to automated systems? How will frustration be handled during the shakedown or adjustment period after the installation of the computer? Each church should thoughtfully analyze and consider the human cost of a church computer.

Social, Ethical, and Moral Questions

Computers in society and the church are also presenting a number of social, ethical, and moral issues. The number of questions in these areas would require another book and an in-depth analysis of such issues would go beyond the scope of this book. The following paragraphs, however, raise one question in each area—social, ethical, moral—so that your computer committee may begin to appreciate the impact of technology upon society.

Unemployment

A major social question related to computers and technology concerns unemployment. It has been documented that hundreds of thousands of unemployed persons throughout the world have had their jobs eliminated by computers. While many companies replacing people power with computer power have provided retraining and relocation services, reports indicate that the majority of businesses do not help in any way those displaced by technology.

For example, telephone companies are now using computers to replace directory assistance (DA) operators. The use of computers, the telephone industry proudly proclaims, reduces the amount of time to respond to a single DA telephone call by two to five seconds. Extrapolated over all calls, the telephone industry will save 20 percent in labor costs for directory assistance calls. This is a cost-effective decision that is common to business and industry, and, in theory, provides beneficial results for the economy. That's fine, but:

- Were current operators asked if they wanted to be replaced by a computer?
- Did the telephone companies offer retraining and absorb them into new jobs?
- Have the telephone companies assisted operators in finding new jobs in other industries if none were available in the telephone industry?
- Related to this issue is the rising cost of telephone services to consumers. Why does the cost of telephone services continue to increase if the telephone industry is so "proud" of the fact they will save 20 percent in labor costs *in this one area alone* by using computers?

These are disturbing questions about computers replacing workers in one common business. While this has occurred in the telephone industry, this industry should not be singled out. *Any* business enterprise that automates should be accountable for the persons they add to the unemployment rolls. If a business replaces one person with a computer, then much of that person's basic identity has been stripped away because American society measures success by jobs and material wealth. In addition, if that business does nothing to help that person find a new job, it then becomes the responsibility of taxpayers to support that unemployed person through the welfare systems.

Even though there is not much Christians can do after the fact other than to support computer-displaced persons, we can look to the future. Churches can become cognizant of companies replacing people with machines and ask such businesses how they will help support the persons being displaced. Churches can also call for the establishment of a public technological displaced persons' fund. Corporations who replace part of their work force with automation would be required to contribute to the fund for supporting those they have made unemployed. The purpose of this fund would be twofold. It could not only help meet the daily needs of the unemployed, but also pay for retraining these persons to develop skills appropriate to survival in a high-tech society.

Another way your church could address this issue is to make the church's computer available for retraining purposes. Many unemployed persons in your community may want to be trained in the use of computers but simply can't afford it because they are out of work. Perhaps someone in the church with computer expertise could volunteer to lead a class for unemployed persons using the church's computer as the training device. Another alternative might be to cooperate with a local continuing education computer class, making the computer available for those in the class. Using your church computer in this way would be a fine ministry to deprived and displaced people seeking to better themselves when they don't have the necessary monetary resources.

Invasion of Privacy

Invasion of privacy is a good ethical question relating to computers. Computers have the tremendous ability to remember minute details about people. Most people really don't know what information about them is maintained by corporations or governments in their computers. If we do take the time to find out what they "have on us" and we find the information is in error, quite often correction is very difficult.

This issue is important for the church because members' data will be loaded into the church's computer. The following questions need to be considered:

- How do church members feel about their "vital statistics" being loaded into the computer?
- Would church members feel they are just numbers in the church's ministry if their information is in the computer?

- What can the study committee do to help the congregation understand that a computer will assist the staff in responding more easily and quickly to their needs?
- What safeguards can the study committee design so that member information in the computer is accurate? For example, a list of information on each church family could be printed each year and distributed to the families for their correction and updating.

Transmission of Values

There are also significant moral questions relating to computers in society and the church. The president of Emory University, Dr. James T. Laney, said in a speech to the United Methodist General Council on Finance and Administration in late 1982 that higher education has lost the ability to transmit *values* to students. Knowledge continues to be transmitted, but values are not.

If this is true, a generation of young people exists today who are not receiving the moral values of society. Yet they are receiving knowledge about how to operate computer systems. Computer crime today is extensive, estimated by some experts to be in the hundreds of millions of dollars. Logically then, if values are not transmitted to society's youth, but knowledge about computers is, will computer crime become as commonplace in the future as fast food is today?

Christians need to seriously contemplate the absence of moral values by asking the following questions:

- If the values of integrity and honesty are not transmitted, how will society's youth use computers when they become adults?
- Will computers be used in the future for political gain or for power struggles? Will they be used to start and sustain wars? Will computers be used for getting ahead in society at the expense of others? Will they be used in more and more criminal activities?

To blame the educational system entirely for this problem is unfair. Our educational institutions are basically a reflection of all society. In other words, every person in society today is responsible for this apparent dilemma. Business people, factory workers, farmers, teachers, parents, pastors, and any other persons with a stake in the world community must accept the blame *and* find solutions to the problem.

The church can help thwart this trend by using its computers in value building and the transmittal of these values. By allowing your church youth to have access to the computer, these issues can be raised and discussed while using the computer as a tool. Software can be developed to explain moral values and lead the church youth in a deeper understanding of the church's mission and ministry. This software could also supplement a parent's or teacher's role in explaining world citizenship responsibilities to church youth.

There are numerous questions revolving around the use of computers in society and the church. While the computer is a tool that can significantly improve ministry, the teachings of Jesus Christ demand that we address some of the social, moral, and ethical questions created by new technologies. From this analysis, the church can learn what its ministry will become in a technologically-dependent, computer-oriented society. Christians can and must learn, by the appropriate use of computers, what discipleship means for the decades and centuries to come.

Epilogue

The epistle of Saint Paul to the Colossians is an ingenious blending of theological doctrine and precepts for daily living. In simple terms, a doctrine is really a teaching about a theoretical concept. A precept is an instruction on using the doctrine (theory) to provide a practical benefit. Both the doctrine and precept are needed, for each draws their life from the other. The doctrine gives birth to the precept and the precept confirms the truth found in the doctrine. Paul counsels that Christian life is an application of these ideals, which often are contradictory and complementary at the same time. The Christian person living in today's world follows a paradoxical combination of theory and practice—of doctrine and precept.

The marriage of Christian theology and computer technology finds its roots in Paul's fusion of doctrine and precept. Colossians 3:1-2 states: "If then you have been raised with Christ, seek the things that are above, where Christ is, seated at the right hand of God. Set your minds on things that are above, not on things that are on earth" (RSV). Everything the church does—from a simple potluck dinner to a complex program of responding to world hunger, from the purchase of paper for a newsletter to the building of a cathedral—cannot be separated from Christ Jesus. The church is the Body of Christ, his visible presence to a hurting, starving world. Any church school paper, benevolent offering, equipment, *or computer* must lead Christians to set their "minds on things that are above, not on things that are on earth." A church computer is not an end itself. It is a means by which Christ's church ministers to the lost, lonely, depressed, hungry, oppressed, and poor.

Computers in the church are merely tools—machines—to support the mission of the church. If this perspective about church computers is not held, the church will become a slave to its information machines. The church will work for the computer rather than the computer working for the church. If the church is not on its guard, computer fascination (though not as violent) will become like the false glory of the Crusades—seeing the things of earth rather than heaven.

The doctrine of church computers is to use them for management information that improves discipleship by providing the church with a new ability to bring Christ to the world and the world to Christ. The cardinal precept for church computers is, on the other hand, a simple result of the doctrine—the computer is *no more and no less* than a tool of ministry. This doctrine/precept is meant to give the church a perspective about computers and other modern technology that it may, with humility, set its corporate mind on "things above."

As a tool, church computers help the Body of Christ to become better stewards of God's gifts. Those gifts are a treasure chest of resources upon which the Body may draw. The most precious of those resources is the Body itself—human beings. The cardinal precept of church computers will free the Body from administering its information to administering its Sacraments where they are desperately needed. It will create a freedom to do the work of Christ in one-to-one ministry rather than by one-to-pencil paperwork. The tool precept, if understood in simplicity, can guide its members to new, exciting, evangelistic ministry in the information age now dawning. When used appropriately, the computer can assist Christ's vineyard workers to discover the ways that will produce a harvest beyond the dreams of even Christ's most faithful servants.

The doctrine of a church computer is to direct the church to "things above" while the precept is to be a simple tool of information management. In the final analysis, the purpose of this book has been to humbly remind the Body of the doctrine and patiently advocate the precept to its distinctive membership. The dawn of a new era in history has begun. Considered carefully, the church computer doctrine and precept will help the Body of Christ to begin with the beginning.

Appendix 1

SOME TECHNICAL CONSIDERATIONS

In any computer, all data and programs are stored in a manner by which the computer can make sense out of them. In general, this information is stored character by character, a character being a single number, letter, or special annotation such as a period, comma, or colon. Table A1-1 displays the valid *printable* characters in any computer. There will also be a number of special printable characters particular to the hardware you are using. In addition, there are a number of *nonprintable* characters, i.e., they don't print on the screen or printer. The nonprintable characters are used by the computer for internal functions.

TABLE A1-1

COMMON PRINTABLE COMPUTER CHARACTERS

A B C D E F G H I J K L M
N O P Q R S T U V W X Y Z

a b c d e f g h i j k l m
n o p q r s t u v w x y z

0 1 2 3 4 5 6 7 8 9

! @ # $ % & * ( ) _ - + = : ;
" ' , . ? / [ ] < >

The Blank

Machine Language

In order to store each of the characters shown in Table A1-1, the computer must have a special designation, or unique way of representing each of the characters. Note that internal code differences exist between upper and lower case letters in the computer. Even a blank between two words on a screen or printer must have an internal representation in the computer. *Machine language* is the name for these combined internal representations. Machine language is a computer language in its most elementary form that is the most efficient for the computer to operate and least efficient for human beings to program. Hence, the name became *machine* language because it is for the machine's benefit.

Machine language is written entirely in the base 2 number system. A base 2 numbering system means that the only valid numbers available for use are "0" and "1." The normal numbering system used in the world today is base 10, meaning that there are ten usable numbers: 0, 1, 2, 3, 4, 5, 6, 7, 8, and 9. The base 2 system uses only two numbers: 0 and 1. It is through the base 2 number system that computers work and represent the numbers and letters everyone uses in daily life.

In the computer world, base 2 numbers are called *binary code* or *binary digits*. Binary code or digits simply means that every single unit in the computer is represented by either 0 or 1. *There are no other numbers in a computer*—only 0's and 1's. Also, a single unit does *not* represent a single character. A single unit (only one binary digit) represents a small piece of any character. In other words, all internal character representations are combinations of only 0's and 1's in very long *strings* or groupings. (A string is a list of binary digits *or* regular characters. Examples: 010111110001011011 or ABCXYZ or the church of Jesus Christ.)

One way to think of this 0 or 1 binary concept is "off" and "on." You turn "on" a light in your kitchen from a switch, or you turn "off" a light from a switch. A "0" could be an "off" state and a "1" could be an "on" state. When the light in your kitchen is "off," it represents a "0" and when it is "on" it represents a "1."

Suppose you are in a room with two lights controlled by two different switches. You can turn the lights off and on to get four of the combinations shown in Table A1-2. Each of these combinations means something different in the way the room is lighted. Each combination casts four different shadows and highlights in the room. In other words, by controlling the two lights from the two switches, you can create four different patterns of light in the room.

Computers are almost exactly like the lighting patterns in our room with two lights controlled from two switches. Computers are composed of electronic circuits that are, in essence, either "off" or "on." As the circuits are turned "off" and "on," different patterns or representations occur in the computer. If a computer had two "lights" or circuits like the example, then it could represent *four* different meanings in its memory.

TABLE A1-2

LIGHTING COMBINATIONS WITH TWO LIGHTS

Light # 1	*Light # 2*
OFF	OFF
ON	OFF
OFF	ON
ON	ON

Another way to understand this is by imagining a bank marquee that constantly flashes the time and temperature. A series of lights flash off and on to form patterns people can understand. This is the essence of a computer memory and how it stores data in machine language. Each light is either illuminated or not—it is either on or off, forming patterns the computer can understand.

Bits and Bytes

A single "light" or "unit" in the computer is called a *bit*. A bit is the most elementary or smallest unit of storage in any computer anywhere in the world. Any bit in any computer regardless of its location or use must equal a 0 or 1. It is not possible to get any smaller in computer representations than a bit. The word *bit* is contracted from the words *bi*nary digi*t*.

To the logical mind, then, how are characters or numbers represented in the computer when a bit must always be a 0 or 1? The numbers 0 or 1 could be represented by a single bit, but what should be done with 2, 3, or any of the other six numbers humanity is accustomed to using? Now consider the letters of the alphabet. The letter "A" could be represented by 0, the letter "B" by 1, but the letter "C" by what? How can the other twenty-four letters of the alphabet be represented in the computer? Finally, how can normal and special punctuation be stored in a computer's memory?

Recall once again the room with the two lights controlled by the two switches. The lights could be "off" or "on" in four combinations, each meaning something different. This is precisely what occurs in a computer, except that 8 bits or lights are used instead of two for internal character representations. By using 8 bits, a total of 128 possible combinations is created thereby representing each of the printable characters in Table A1-1 and the necessary nonprintable characters.

A string or series of 8 bits in the computer is a *byte*. (This is pronounced like the word *bite*.) These 8 bits form in various combinations to make numbers, letters, special characters, and the blank space. In most computers it takes 8 bits or 1 byte for every individual character. In other words: 1 byte = 1 character. Every time you press a key on the computer's keyboard, an 8-bit character byte representing the key you touched is generated and placed into the computer's memory.

Units of Mass Storage

You will frequently hear the terms *K* or *mega-byte* (MB) used by vendors and others who discuss computers. These are two terms used to designate large amounts of storage. They are always used in conjunction with computer memory sizes.

A K equals 1,024 bytes of storage. In computerese slang, a K is used to mean 1,000 bytes or characters of storage. Thus, when someone says that a computer has 64K of RAM, they mean that a certain machine has about 64,000 characters of active, internal, core memory. If a person says their computer has 128K, they mean it has about 128,000 internal memory bytes.

A mega-byte means 1,000,000 characters of storage. Thus, when a certain computer has 1.2MB of floppy disk storage, it has 1,200,000 bytes or characters of mass storage on the floppies. This would be equivalent to about two hundred twenty-five pages of single spaced 8½ x 11 typed sheets with normal margins and about fifty lines to a page. If a computer has a 20MB hard disk, then 20,000,000 characters of storage are available in that machine.

In the future, even larger amounts of storage will be possible on the microcomputers used in the church. Someday it will be commonplace to have a *giga-byte* (GB) of storage on small computers. One GB is the same as 1,000,000,000 characters or bytes of storage. In the future, GB storage devices will provide the most cost-effective type of mass storage for computers.

Some Odds and Ends about Bits and Bytes

As you have probably guessed, the performing world of bits and bytes consists of a cast of literally millions. The enormity of bits and bytes in even a small computer can be almost too great to comprehend. For example, in a computer with 128K memory, there are 1,024,000 individual bits. On a 75MB disk, i.e., seventy-five million characters, there are 600,000,000 individual bits, "flashing" off and on at rates that approach the speed of light!

A more realistic bits and bytes example is your name. If your name is twenty characters in length, it takes 160 individual bits, all 0's and 1's, so that the computer can make sense out of it!

It may be of interest to you that in the earliest days of computers, *all* programming was done in machine language. Everything was programmed in 0's and 1's. When a *bug* (program error) occurred, it was virtually impossible to find the problem. The programmer almost always started over and hoped he or she could correct the error the second time—or third time—or fourth time—etc. The cast of millions was certainly confusing then. Fortunately, today the computer does the translation into machine language and allows human beings to program in BASIC and other higher level languages. This means that the bugs are much easier to correct.

Standard Computer Codes

In the early days of computers, it was felt that some standards were needed for the 8-bit combinations. In other words, a common alphabet was needed so computers and the people who ran them could talk more easily with one another. The result was two standard alphabets or codes.

The first of these codes is called *ASCII*. ASCII is an acronym for the "American Standard Code for Information Interchange." This code is used by all computer manufacturers except IBM.

ASCII consists of an 8-bit byte, or 8-bit combinations representing various characters. This code has a total of one hundred twenty-eight characters in its alphabet. ASCII is the most common computer code found among the small computers that would fulfill a church's requirements. Table A1-3 lists the ASCII code set for your future reference.

The other major computer character code or alphabet used

today is *EBCDIC*. These letters represent the "Extended Binary Coded Decimal Interchange Code."

EBCDIC has a 9-bit byte, or 9-bit combinations representing various characters. This code has a total of 256 bit patterns or characters in its alphabet. This code was invented by the IBM corporation and is used in all their computers. Table A1-4 lists the EBCDIC code set.

Because there are two standard code sets, transferring data between IBM and non-IBM computers requires special considerations. If you ever have occasion to transfer church data from an IBM computer to a non-IBM computer, or vice versa, you must be aware of the internal code differences. At some point, a translation or *conversion* from ASCII to EBCDIC or EBCDIC to ASCII must be made to complete the transfer. You do not need to program the computers for these differences, but you will need to purchase special software that can do the translation. This software is frequently called *protocol* communications programs, which allow the two computers to transfer information efficiently through the two codes.

TABLE A1-3

AMERICAN
STANDARD CODE
FOR INFORMATION
INTERCHANGE
(ASCII)

The ASCII computer alphabet uses an 8-bit code where bit number 8 is the "control" bit. Bit 8 is usually called the parity bit, high order bit, or low order bit. The remaining 7 bits are used for representing the character. Bit 8 is always the first bit in the sequence and bit 1 is the last. Bit 8 is not shown below because it depends upon the control system being used. Nonprintable characters are listed first.

Nonprintable ASCII Characters:

Character	7-bit Code	Meaning
NUL	0000000	Null Signal
SOH	0000001	Start of Heading
STX	0000010	Start of Text
ETX	0000011	End of Text
EOT	0000100	End of Transmission
ENQ	0000101	Enquiry
ACK	0000110	Acknowledge
BEL	0000111	Bell (audible signal)
BS	0001000	Backspace
HT	0001001	Horizontal Tabulation
LF	0001010	Line Feed
VT	0001011	Vertical Tabulation
FF	0001100	Form Feed
CR	0001101	Carriage Return
SO	0001110	Shift Out
SI	0001111	Shift In
DLE	0010000	Data Link Escape
DC1	0010001	Device Control 1
DC2	0010010	Device Control 2
DC3	0010011	Device Control 3
DC4	0010100	Device Control 4
NAK	0010101	Negative Acknowledgment
SYN	0010110	Synchronous Idle
ETB	0010111	End of Transmission Block
CAN	0011000	Cancel
EM	0011001	End of Medium
SUB	0011010	Substitute
ESC	0011011	Escape
FS	0011100	File Separator
GS	0011101	Group Separator
RS	0011110	Record Separator
US	0011111	Unit Separator
DEL	1111111	Delete

Printable ASCII Characters:

Character	7-bit Code	Character	7-bit Code
A	1000001	w	1110111
B	1000010	x	1111000
C	1000011	y	1111001
D	1000100	z	1111010
E	1000101	0	0110000
F	1000110	1	0110001
G	1000111	2	0110010
H	1001000	3	0110011
I	1001001	4	0110100
J	1001010	5	0110101
K	1001011	6	0110110
L	1001100	7	0110111
M	1001101	8	0111000
N	1001110	9	0111001
O	1001111	!	0100001
P	1010000	"	0100010
Q	1010001	#	0100011
R	1010010	$	0100100
S	1010011	%	0100101
T	1010100	&	0100110
U	1010101	'	0110111
V	1010110	(	0101000
W	1010111	)	0101001
X	1011000	*	0101010
Y	1011001	+	0101011
Z	1011010	,	0101100
a	1100001	-	0101101
b	1100010	.	0101110
c	1100011	/	0101111
d	1100100	:	0111010
e	1100101	;	0111011
f	1100110	<	0111100
g	1100111	=	0111101
h	1101000	>	0111110
i	1101001	?	0111111
j	1101010	[	1011011

Character	7-bit Code	Character	7-bit Code
k	1101011	]	1011101
l	1101100	\	1011100
m	1101101	^	1011110
n	1101110	_	1011111
o	1101111	{	1111011
p	1110000	}	1111101
q	1110001	`	1100000
r	1110010	|	1111100
s	1110011	~	1111110
t	1110100	@	1000000
u	1110101	BLANK	0100000
v	1110110		

TABLE A1-4

EXTENDED BINARY CODED
DECIMAL INTERCHANGE CODE
(EBCDIC)

The EBCDIC computer alphabet uses a 9-bit code where bit number 9 is the "control" bit. Bit 9 is usually called the parity bit. The remaining 8 bits are used for representing the character. Bit 9 is always the first bit in the sequence and bit 1 is the last. Bit 9 is not shown below because it depends upon the control system being used. Nonprintable characters are listed first.

Nonprintable EBCDIC Characters:

Character	8-bit Code	Meaning
NUL	00000000	Null Signal
SOH	00000001	Start of Heading
STX	00000010	Start of Text
ETX	00000011	End of Text
EOT	00110111	End of Transmission

Character	8-bit Code	Meaning
ENQ	00101101	Enquiry
ACK	00101110	Acknowledge
BEL	00101111	Bell (audible signal)
BS	00010110	Backspace
HT	00000101	Horizontal Tabulation
LF	00100101	Line Feed
VT	00001011	Vertical Tabulation
FF	00001100	Form Feed
CR	00001101	Carriage Return
NL	00010101	New Line
SO	00001110	Shift Out
SI	00001111	Shift In
DLE	00010000	Data Link Escape
DC1	00010001	Device Control 1
DC2	00010010	Device Control 2
DC3	00010011	Device Control 3
DC4	00111100	Device Control 4
NAK	00111101	Negative Acknowledgment
SYN	00110010	Synchronous Idle
ETB	00100110	End of Transmission Block
CAN	00011000	Cancel
EM	00011001	End of Medium
SUB	00111111	Substitute
ESC	00100111	Escape
FS	00011100	File Separator
GS	00011101	Group Separator
RS	00011110	Record Separator
US	00011111	Unit Separator
DEL	00000111	Delete

Printable EBCDIC Characters (some variations occur depending upon the computer involved):

Character	8-bit Code	Character	8-bit Code
A	11000001	w	10100110
B	11000010	x	10100111
C	11000011	y	10101000
D	11000100	z	10101001
E	11000101	0	11110000
F	11000110	1	11110001
G	11000111	2	11110010
H	11001000	3	11110011
I	11001001	4	11110100
J	11010001	5	11110101
K	11010010	6	11110110
L	11010011	7	11110111
M	11010100	8	11111000
N	11010101	9	11111001
O	11010110	!	11010000
P	11010111	"	01111111
Q	11011000	#	01111011
R	11011001	$	01011011
S	11100010	%	01101100
T	11100011	&	01010000
U	11100100	'	01111101
V	11100101	(	01001101
W	11100100	)	01011101
X	11100111	*	01011100
Y	11101000	+	01001110
Z	11101001	´	01101011
a	10000001	@	01111100
b	10000010	.	01001011
c	10000011	/	01100001
d	10000100	:	01111010
e	10000101	;	01011110
f	10000110	<	01001100
g	10000111	=	01111110
h	10001000	>	01101110
i	10001001	?	01101111

Character	8-bit Code	Character	8-bit Code
j	10010001	[	01001010
k	10010010	]	01011010
l	10010011	\	11100000
m	10010100	Center Dot	01111001
n	10010101	__	01101101
o	10010110	I	01001111
p	10010111	BLANK	01000000
q	10011000		
r	10011001		
s	10100010		
t	10100011		
u	10100100		
v	10100101		

Data Flow Paths

Each time you press a key on the hardware keyboard, an 8-bit or 9-bit code is generated in the computer. This code means something to the computer. It communicates a message to the machine so it can process the information into the desired form. The computer interprets each byte or series of bytes in different ways to produce the result needed. In other words, data moves or travels electronically through the various pieces of hardware (input, output, CPU) based upon the instructions provided in the software.

The flow of data in a computer follows a variety of paths depending upon the particular function being attempted. In order to assist your church with its work, the computer moves data in three basic ways. Each of these is described in the following paragraphs.

The simplest flow of data in a computer occurs when the operator enters a letter on the keyboard and it displays on the screen. For example, if the key marked with the letter "A" is pressed, the byte that represents "A" will be generated in the computer's CPU memory. The CPU then transmits the byte to the CRT (screen) and it appears as an "A" so that the operator can visually read it. Diagram A1-5 illustrates this process.

The second way data is manipulated involves the computer's mass storage device(s). This data flow path is more complicated than the previous and is illustrated in Diagram A1-6.

In this data flow path, the operator types a command into the computer requesting that a certain piece of information be displayed on the screen. However, this information is located on one of the computer's floppy disks. An example of this would be when a church member moves and the address information must be updated.

Diagram A1-5

INFORMATION FROM KEYBOARD TO SCREEN

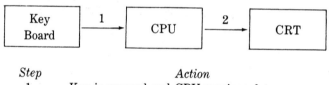

Step	Action
1.	Key is pressed and CPU receives data.
2.	CPU processes and sends data to the CRT.

The command is typed by the operator into the computer. The command is then placed in the CPU memory where it is properly interpreted. If the CPU "decides" it is a valid command, the disk is then directed to send the proper information. The disk drive responds by turning the disk to the correct location, reading the data from the disk, and transmitting the member's name and address to the CPU. The CPU verifies that the information has been correctly received and sends it to the screen. The screen then displays the data originally requested by the operator and the computer waits for further instructions. If everything works properly, this process will take about one second.

A combination of the two data flow paths in Diagrams A1-5

and A1-6 would be used when a new church member's name and address need to be entered into the computer. The name and address would be typed, displayed, and verified by the operator. Then the computer would place the new information into a vacant space on the disk. The operator does not need to know the available spaces on the disk for the information. The CPU manages this process.

Diagram A1-6

INFORMATION FROM DISK TO SCREEN

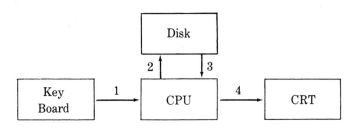

Step	Action
1.	Command is entered, received by CPU, and interpreted.
2.	CPU directs the disk to send the requested information.
3.	Disk sends data to the CPU. CPU verifies its proper receipt.
4.	CPU sends data to CRT where it is displayed.

The third data flow path is the most complex of the three basic ones important to church work. This path is shown in Diagram A1-7. An example of this process is when a report of the current month and year-to-date member's giving is to be printed onto paper. In this operation, the necessary command is typed, the pledge accounting disk *file* is located, and the information is printed onto paper by the computer's printer. (A file in the computer is much like a file in a filing cabinet. It contains information relevant to a particular subject.)

Diagram A1-7

INFORMATION FROM DISK TO PRINTER AND SCREEN

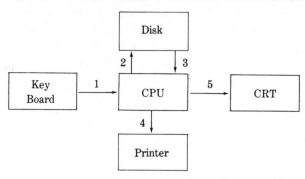

Step	*Action*
1.	Command is entered, received by CPU, and interpreted.
2.	CPU directs the disk to send the requested information.
3.	Disk sends data to the CPU. CPU verifies its proper receipt.
4.	CPU sends data to printer where it is printed.
5.	CPU *may* also send data to CRT where it is displayed as it sends the data to the printer.

This process begins with the operator entering the appropriate command on the keyboard. The command is then placed into the CPU memory and interpreted. The CPU directs the disk to send it the first name and address in the pledge accounting file. The disk responds by sending the proper *record* to the CPU. The CPU then manipulates the information into the form programmed by the software. After this, the data is sent by the CPU to the printer where it is printed onto the paper. Each time a name, address, and pledge accounting information are printed, the CPU directs the disk to send another record until the entire file has been printed. (A record contains information about one family in the pledge accounting file. Each record might contain name, address, yearly pledge, year-to-date contributions, etc. In other words, every computer file is composed of many records relating to a particular subject.)

In an operation such as this one, it is often desirable to have something appear on the screen as each record is printed. This is not absolutely necessary, but frequently this feature is already programmed into the software. When this is true, the CPU will send data to the screen at almost exactly the same moment that the pledge record is sent to the printer. For example, while the pledge record #26 may be printing, the screen may also show "now printing record #26." This is useful in certain situations, but will decrease the efficiency and speed of the printing operation.

Single-Task and Multi-Task Computers

The above three data flow paths primarily relate to microcomputers. However, more complicated flow paths occur in larger computers. While the basics of data flow described above exist in the larger machines, many functions are supported at once. This is *not* true in most average microcomputers. They are designed as *single-task* machines. A single-task computer is one that can complete only one function at a time. In other words, when the monthly pledge accounting report is printing, the computer is dedicated to that task and cannot be used for anything else.

Larger computers are *multi-task*, which means they can work on numerous functions simultaneously. For example, a multi-task computer can print the monthly pledge accounting report, receive new member data, and edit the pastor's sermon through word processing all at one time. A multi-task computer does this through several *terminals* attached to the CPU. The terminals all have access to the CPU at the same time.

A terminal is an input/output device that allows a person to communicate with the computer. A terminal can be a microcomputer, or it may be just a keyboard and screen. A terminal also can be a keyboard attached to a printer that acts just like a screen does.

Diagram A1-8 shows a simple schematic of a multi-task computer *configuration* with data flow indicated by the arrows. Most churches do not need a multi-task computer as their first machine; however, after several years of a computer operation a multi-task machine may be necessary.

Modems

Diagram A1-8 shows another hardware device not previously discussed. This is the *modem,* which means "modulate/demodulate." Modems are necessary to use your computer over telephone lines. If the church desires to access large commercial data bases through their computer, a modem is required. If you wish to transfer church data from one computer to another church computer, you must have a modem. In addition, the computer at the other end must also have a modem. Two modems are required whenever any computer device uses a telephone line—one at each end of the line. Your church is responsible for the modem at your end. Other computer owners are responsible for the modems at their end.

Modems can either be rented or purchased. Most local telephone companies will rent a modem to an organization for a monthly fee. The rental fee is added to your regular telephone bill each month. You can also purchase a modem from your computer vendor or local computer store. Economically, if the church rents a modem, the rental fees will essentially pay for the modem in about one to two years. For example, if a modem costs $300 to purchase, and an equivalent modem can be rented for $25 a month, the rental fees will pay for the initial cost of the modem in one year.

Modems come in various speeds, and the speed of the

Diagram A1-8

TYPICAL MULTI-TASK COMPUTER CONFIGURATION

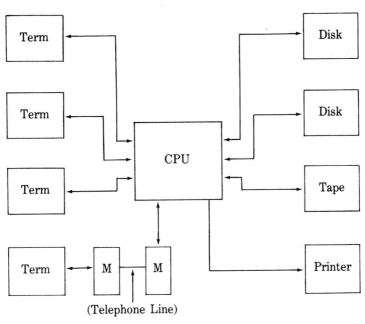

(Telephone Line)

Key: CPU..........Central Processing Unit (I/O), memory usually expressed in "K" or "Meg" (1 Meg = 1 MB).

Disk..........Disk drive device (I/O), memory usually expressed in "MB" or "GB."

M..............Modem, modulate/demodulate device (I/O). (Modems allow computers to use telephone lines.)

Printer.......Dot matrix, letter quality, or line printer (O). (Multi-task computers can support several printers of differing types.)

Tape..........Tape drive device (I/O).

Term.........Terminal (I/O).

Note: I/O = Input and output device.
O = Output device only.

modems must be matched at each end of the telephone line in order for them to work. The most common speeds for modems are 300 *baud* and 1200 baud. Modems also come in speeds slower than 300 baud and in speeds up to 56,000 baud. Low-speed modems are not cost effective in almost all instances. Also, high-speed modems are very expensive and are used only for very high-volume data transfers in business and government. A 300 or 1200 baud modem is sufficient for your church. (Baud is a slang term for *bps* or bits per second.)

If you rent, you will need to ask the telephone company for either a 103A or 212A modem. The 103A modem gives 300 baud speed. The 212A provides both 300 and 1200 baud, and therefore is the more versatile. If the church purchases a modem, the vendor may want to know the equivalency rating to the telephone system. If you want a 300 baud modem, you tell the vendor that the church needs a 103A equivalent modem. If you want both the 300 and 1200 baud capabilities, then you should indicate a 212A equivalent modem is needed. In general, the 300/1200 baud is usually more expensive *initially* than a 300 baud modem, but less expensive in the long term.

You may be wondering why a modem with both 300 and 1200 baud capability would ever be needed. A modem of 1200 baud is four times faster than 300 baud, which means you can reduce the telephone time necessary to access a large data base or "talk" with another church computer by almost 75 percent. This means that your telephone bill will be less. On the other hand, many smaller computers owned by individuals and even some public data bases have *only* the 300 baud capability. If you purchase a modem with both 300 and 1200 baud capacities, the church wll have the best of two worlds—lower cost when possible, and the ability to communicate with slower speed computers.

Even though the 300/1200 baud modem may save you 75 percent in telephone time on the faster speed, it may, in fact, cost you *more* money depending upon the computer you are accessing. For example, a public data base may charge $24 an hour to use their computer at 300 baud. On the other hand, they may charge $72 an hour to use their computer at 1200 baud. Suppose you make a call to the computer at 300 baud and it takes one hour. At 1200 baud, the same call would probably take about thirty minutes maximum allowing for human "think" time and options selection while signed onto the computer. Table A1-9 shows the results of this.

TABLE A1-9

DATA BASE ACCESS COST COMPARISONS

Baud Rate	Rate for Access	Length of Call	Cost of Access	Cost of Call	Total Cost
300	$24/hr.	1 hour	$24.00	$5.00	$29.00
1200	$72/hr.	½ hour	$36.00	$2.50	$38.50

As Table A1-9 points out, even though you may have a faster speed modem, your total cost may be higher. This will depend upon the computers the church may desire to use, and the data they are providing to the church. Thus, the faster modem may reduce telephone time, but increase overall cost. The church may feel the reduced telephone time is a large enough benefit to justify an increased cost for access to certain data bases. Generally, however, the faster baud modem is more cost effective in most instances.

Modems are also available in straight 1200 baud. This type of modem is good, but limiting because so many of the smaller computers use 300 baud. Thus, your church could obtain a modem with 1200 baud only, but be prepared not to have access to some desirable computer services.

Operating Systems

You have probably observed that much of what occurs in a computer revolves directly around the CPU, which controls the flow of information in the machine and handles all necessary functions in order to make it work. In many ways, the CPU is the chief administrator of the computer, providing all guidance and leadership to the other components.

It is natural, however, to wonder how the CPU works. Precisely what makes the CPU do what it is supposed to do? All CPU functions are maintained by a vendor supplied software package called the *operating system*. The operating system resides in the CPU's memory, was written by a human being, and gives the computer its ability to be a useful tool.

The operating system uses a certain portion of the CPU memory and leaves the rest available for you. This means that if a computer has 64K of RAM memory and 24K is needed by the operating system, then you have 40K available for your work. This limitation is crucial when purchasing software from a vendor or computer store. If the software you are purchasing needs 48K to function, but you have only 40K of user memory, then the software won't work on the computer. Thus, it is important to know how much memory is used by the operating system so that allowances can be · made for applications software.

In the microcomputer world, as many operating systems exist as do manufacturers. The most common operating systems today are called CP/M, CP/M-86, MS-DOS, and Unix. Most applications or user software on microcomputers is being developed around these particular operating systems.

The CP/M operating system is common to the 8-bit *architecture* computers. This is often referred to as an "8-bit processor," or 8-bit microcomputer. The CP/M-86, MS-DOS, and Unix operating systems are common to the 16-bit and 32-bit microcomputers. The bit architecture of a computer refers to the number of bits and bytes the CPU can handle in a given number of *microseconds* (μs) or *nanoseconds* (ηs). (1 μs = 1/1,000,000 of a second; 1 ηs = 1/1,000,000,000 of a second.)

Theoretically, if a person purchases a CP/M based software package from a local computer store and loads it into a computer that uses the CP/M operating system, the software would operate. Likewise, if another church develops software on a CP/M computer, your church should be able to use it on your computer. In reality, this is not always true simply because vendors design idiosyncrasies into their computer to corner a certain part of the computer market. As a result, your church may purchase a CP/M based financial software package that will operate on an ABC computer, but not on a an XYZ computer even though both computers use CP/M. In other words, operating systems may be generally common to many computers, but not fully standardized to allow for the easy interchange of software between computers.

Regardless of the minor differences between computers, churches should consider software and hardware written under one of the common operating systems. This will allow for a relatively easy exchange of software between churches and provide better long-term support. In addition, new software developments will usually occur in the common operating systems, therefore allowing the church to take advantage of new ideas in an inexpensive way. In the final analysis, a church using a common operating system will be able to use the latest in modern computer software technology.

Appendix 2

GLOSSARY OF COMPUTER TERMS

Definitions of many common computer terms are listed below. The number(s) in parentheses following each definition indicate the chapter or appendix where the term is described in detail.

Architecture—The electronic and hardware design of a computer (appendix 1).

ASCII—American Standard Code for Information Interchange; the internal code used by all computers except IBM (appendix 1).

Back-up—A procedure that produces a copy of all information maintained in the computer (11).

Baud—See "bps."

Binary code (binary digits)—A code that makes use of only 0's or 1's (appendix 1).

Binary digits (binary code)—See "Binary code."

Bit—The smallest unit of storage; always equal to 0 or 1; 8 bits = 1 byte; comes from the words "*bi*nary dig*it*" (4, appendix 1).

bps—The speed of data transmission over a telephone line; usually used in conjunction with "modem" (appendix 1).

Bug—A software error (appendix 1).

Byte—A unit of storage; 1 byte = 1 character; 1 byte = 8 bits (4, appendix 1).

Cathode Ray Tube (CRT, VDT, Video Display Tube)—A television type monitor or terminal (4).

Central Processing Unit (CPU)—The controlling device that provides the necessary electronic information in order that all software and hardware may achieve their specified functions (4).

Computer—A machine or device composed of logical electronic circuits designed to generate desired output in a specified sequence from a logical set of instructions as produced by a given set of input data (4).

Configuration—A description and/or diagram of the major components in a hardware or software system (6, appendix 1).

Conversion—A procedure to change computer information in one coding scheme into another (appendix 1).

Core memory—A specialized device found only in the CPU designed to store data related to the CPU's specific functions (4).

cps—Character per second; usually used when referring to printer speeds (4, 9).

CRT (Cathode Ray Tube, VDT, Video Display Tube)—See "Central Processing Unit."

CPU (Central Processing Unit)—See "Cathode Ray Tube."

Cyberphobia—Fear of computers (2, 15).

Data base—A series of integrated computer files containing information relating to one or several subjects; usually data bases can be accessed by many persons and organizations (10).

Data Processing (DP)—The action of receiving information, processing it, and outputting into a specified form (3).

Documentation—Written materials that describe hardware and/or software (8, 9, 10).

Dot matrix printer—A printer that outputs information using pixels (dots) to form the characters; the output is not letter quality (4, 9).

Double density—A method of storing data on a floppy disk; results in a greater number of characters on the disk (9).

DP (Data Processing)—See "Data Processing."

Drive—A device that inputs and outputs information to and from a mass storage magnetic medium such as a floppy or hard disk (4).

Dual-side floppy disk—A floppy disk with two logical sides (9).

EBCDIC—Extended Binary Coded Decimal Interchange Code; the internal code used by IBM computers (appendix 1).

EDP (Electronic Data Processing)—See "Electronic Data Processing."

Electronic Data Processing (EDP)—The action of utilizing an electronic tool to facilitate data processing (3).

File—Contains information relevant to a particular subject; files are stored on disks and tapes (appendix 1).

Floppy disk—A mass storage magnetic media common to microcomputers; they come in different sizes, densities, and with one or two sides (4, 9).

GB (Giga-byte)—See "Giga-byte."

Giga-byte (GB)—One billion bytes of storage (appendix 1).

GIGO—Garbage In/Garbage Out (2).

Hard disk—A mass storage magnetic media that is very fast and cost effective (4).

Hardware—The physical or tangible parts of any computer that occupy space (4).

Input device—Provides the function of placing data and programs into the computer (4).

Interface—The ways and levels of efficiency in which hardware connects with other hardware and/or software links with other software (8).

K—1,024 bytes of storage; often shortened to 1,000 bytes of storage for simplicity (4, appendix 1).

Keypunch—A typewriter-like device used to cut holes into punched cards (4).

Language—A comprehensive set of signs, symbols, and commands that allows a human being to communicate with a computer, and is used by a programmer to create a computer program (4).

Letter quality printer—A printer that outputs information in typewriter quality (4, 9).

lpm (lines per minute)—Usually used when referring to printer speeds (4).

Machine language—A computer language in its most elementary form that represents characters through a scheme of only 0's and 1's (appendix 1).

Management Information System (MIS)—Systematized data that is both internal and external to an organization used to generate more effective and efficient administration of the organization (3).

Mass storage device—Provides the function of storage of large amounts of data or information for instant retrieval on a magnetic medium. Examples: floppy disk drive; hard disk drive; cassette tape drive, etc. (4).

MB (Megabyte)—See "Megabyte."

Megabyte—One million bytes of storage; synonym: "Meg" (4, appendix 1).

Memory—A device or devices in which information is stored (4).

Menu—A list of items presented on the computer's monitor from which the operator makes a choice before the program continues (8).

Microsecond (μs)—One one-millionth of a second, i.e., 1/1,000,000 of a second; designated by "μs" (appendix 1).

MIS (Management Information System)—See "Management Information System."

Modem—A device to allow data communications over standard telephone lines. Means modulate/demodulate (appendix 1).

Multi-task computer—A computer capable of completing many functions simultaneously (appendix 1).

Nanosecond (ηs)—One one-billionth of a second, i.e., 1/1,000,000,000 of a second; designated by "ηs" (appendix 1).

ηs (nanosecond)—See "Nanosecond."

On line—All the data and software that is available to the user at any one moment without loading a different disk or tape (8).

Operating system—A software package that controls all internal computer functions; it is provided by the vendor (appendix 1).

Output device—Prints or displays data in a form desired by the user (4).

Peripheral—A hardware device connected to a CPU that provides a specific function; examples: disk drive, terminal, etc. (12).

Pixel—A very small mechanical dot that when used with other pixels will print characters onto paper; used with dot matrix printers (9).

Printer—An output device that prints information onto paper (4).

Program (software)—See "Software."

Programmer—A person who writes computer programs (4).

Programming—The art or skill of writing a program for the computer (4).

Prompt—A question printed on the monitor that requires an operator response before the program continues (8).

Protocol—A standard that allows two different computers to transfer information efficiently (appendix 1).

Punched card—A stiff paper card with holes punched in certain patterns used to input data into a computer. This is an older technology rapidly disappearing (4).

Punched card reader—An input device designed to "read" punched cards (4).

RAM (Random Access Memory)—See "Random Access Memory."

Random Access Memory (RAM)—A computer's core memory that can be accessed by the user (4).

Read Only Memory (ROM)—A computer's core memory that cannot be normally accessed by the user (4).

Record—Contains information related to one grouping, e.g., name, address, yearly pledge, date of baptism, etc.; a "file" is composed of many records (appendix 1).

ROM (Read Only Memory)—See "Read Only Memory."

Single density—A method of storing data on a floppy disk; results in a smaller number of characters on the disk (9).

Single-side floppy disk—A floppy disk with one logical side (9).

Single-task computer—A computer capable of completing only one function at any given moment (appendix 1).

Software (program)—A logical sequence or set of instructions written in a computer language designed to achieve a specific purpose (2, 4).

Software package—A set of two or more interfaced programs designed for a specific purpose (4).

String—A list of characters (appendix 1).

Terminal—An input/output device that allows communication between a human being and a computer (appendix 1).

Turnkey system—A combination of hardware and software usually sold at special discount prices (8).

μs (microsecond)—See "Microsecond."

User friendly—Hardware and software that is easy to use from the operator's point of view (2, 8).

VDT (Video Display Tube, CRT, Cathode Ray Tube)—See "Cathode Ray Tube" (4).

Video Display Tube (VDT, CRT, Cathode Ray Tube)—See "Cathode Ray Tube" (4).

Word Processing—The manipulation of characters, words, phrases, paragraphs, and pages of text so that letters, reports, and other printed documents are produced in an easy and efficient manner (3).

Index

154